MW01098216

Learn CS Concepts
with

Scratch

4th edition

Create exciting games and animation in Scratch
and learn Computer Science principles

Abhay B. Joshi

Book series on "Learning computer programming and CS principles"

To Seymour Papert who inspired me to take this path

All rights reserved by the author

Published by:
SPARK Institute and Publications
16668 NE 121st STREET
Redmond, WA 98052, USA
1st edition: 26 January 2017
2nd edition: 5 October 2017
3rd edition: 15 July 2018
4th edition: 5 October 2022

Cover design by:
Ravindra Pande

To order your digital copy:
Go to Amazon.com

To order your printed copy:
Go to Amazon.com or write to: abjoshi@yahoo.com
Check pricing at: http://www.abhayjoshi.net/mybooks/bscratch.pdf

Other books in this series:
Advanced Scratch Programming
Pen Art in Scratch Programming

Click http://www.abhayjoshi.net/mybooks/csseries.pdf to see the complete list.

Preface

*It [so] happens that the process of programming a computer is very appealing
to many kids; by taking that process seriously, they experience the sort of
commitment and pursuit of excellence that other kids get from
team sports, from the school newspaper, and so on.*
– Brian Harvey, CS Professor, UC Berkeley

Background

I started writing this book as a supplement for the projects covered in another book titled "Advanced Scratch Programming", which requires you to be familiar with a variety of CS (Computer Science) and Scratch concepts. From a mere supplement, this work has now evolved into a full, introductory, self-study tutorial in which you will learn all these concepts through a series of exciting projects and programming activities.

The idea of using *computer programming as a medium for learning* is rapidly gaining acceptance. The benefits of learning programming and *computer science* concepts well before college – even in elementary grades – are well-understood.

Here is a list of some of the amazing things that happen when children and young adults engage in computer programming:

- They become *active* and *creative* learners, because they explore ideas through a hands-on activity with an infinitely powerful tool.
- They learn to think about and analyze *their own thinking*, because that is the only way to program computers.
- They learn to solve complex problems by breaking them into smaller sub-problems.

- They learn a new way of thinking (called "computational" thinking).
- In the world of programming, answers are not simply "right" or "wrong"; this prepares a student's mindset for real-life problems.
- The learning process is transformed from *acquiring facts* to *thinking creatively and analytically*.

About this interactive book

The choice of programming language is critical to achieve the intended objectives of teaching CS to beginners. In this book we use the Scratch programming language. Scratch is an entertaining and powerful language, and yet it is easy to learn. It is known as a "low floor and high ceiling" language – it allows the learner to build his/her vocabulary without getting mired in the complexities of syntax and grammar.

There is a lot of material on Scratch Programming on the Internet, including videos, online courses, Scratch projects, and so on. This book is meant to offer a more organized and tutorial-like treatment to learning Scratch. It is also focused more on learning CS concepts rather than Scratch itself.

In short, this book is for students who are keen to learn CS concepts and have no prior programming background.

I call this an "interactive book" because it is something between a traditional book – which is static and passive – and a fully interactive online course. It does look like a book: it has a series of chapters, diagrams, a lot of text, etc. But it also contains links to online Scratch programs, code snippets, references, which the reader is expected to click and explore to fully benefit from the ideas presented.

How the book is organized

The book is organized as a series of units – each containing a bunch of CS concepts and associated programming activities. Typically, each unit also includes a major programming project that helps you practice all the concepts learnt till then. Answers to all "review questions" and links to working programs for most of the programming exercises in the book are available online. Download them at: http://abhayjoshi.net/scratch/book0/Solutions.pdf.

Additional Scratch Material

The Internet is replete with study material, videos, and courses on Scratch and Computer Science. I have listed below a few general Internet-based references that you could use to study Scratch and CS concepts in more detail.

Scratch Offline Editor:

This editor itself offers help on every feature of Scratch. Click on the "?" symbol in the upper right corner to open this help. You will find step-by-step tutorials, how-to guides, and explanation of every command block of Scratch.

Scratch Website (scratch.mit.edu):

This website is an authentic source of information related to Scratch. Click on the "Help" button to access user guides, frequently asked questions, help with scripts, and video tutorials.

ScratchEd Website (scratched.gse.harvard.edu):

This website is an online community for educators and it offers stories, discussions, and resources such as the Scratch curriculum guide.

Scratch Wiki Website (wiki.scratch.mit.edu):

This website contains a wide variety of articles by Scratchers for Scratchers, including advanced topics and tutorials.

YouTube videos:

There are literally hundreds of YouTube videos that you can view to understand basic concepts of Scratch. On the YouTube website, search for "Scratch programming" to get a list of useful videos.

Hardware and Software

This book has been designed for Scratch version 3. Download Scratch 3 editor at: http://scratch.mit.edu. Scratch offline editor works on all Windows, Linux, and Mac computers.

You may also work online by creating your own account at http://scratch.mit.edu as long as it supports Scratch version 3.

Acknowledgements

Most of the material used for this book came from my teaching experience of the last several years. I would like to thank Aksharnandan School in Pune for allowing me to teach Scratch to their students every year (since 2008) during my summer visits to Pune. I wish to thank my 1000+ students. They tolerated my ideas, contributed their own, and frankly told me what was interesting and what wasn't. Their projects were amazingly creative – which only reinforced my belief that teaching programming is a good idea!

I wish to thank Tanuja Joshi for reviewing the material of this book diligently and tirelessly and for providing me with valuable suggestions. I wish to thank Ravindra Pande for creating a truly beautiful cover for the book.

Finally, this book would not have been possible without the constant encouragement of my friends and family.

I do hope that you will find this book useful and enjoyable.

Abhay B. Joshi (abjoshi@yahoo.com)
Seattle, USA
5 October 2017

Author's background

As a freelance teacher, Abhay's area of interest is teaching Computer Programming as "the exciting new magic" and also as "a medium for learning" in the constructivist tradition. He has been teaching regularly to elementary, middle, and high school students in WA, USA and Pune, India since 2008. He teaches at Aksharnandan School in Pune, India every summer, and works with TEALS (http://tealsk12.org/) to teach Computer Science to high school students in the US. Abhay teaches both in person and over the Internet using video-conferencing tools. Since 2011, he has authored or co-authored several programming books, which are based on Scratch, Snap, and Logo. He has written several articles to promote CS education, and offers teacher-training workshops to encourage aspiring teachers to experiment with this idea.

Abhay has been associated with the Software Industry since 1988 as a programmer, product developer, entrepreneur, and teacher. After getting an MS in Computer Engineering from Syracuse University (USA), he worked as a software engineer for product companies that developed operating systems, network protocols, and secure software. In 1997, Abhay co-founded Disha Technologies, which grew to become a successful software services organization.

Programming remains one of Abhay's favorite hobbies, and he continues to explore the "entertaining, intellectual, and educational" aspects of programming.

In my vision, the child programs the computer, and in doing so, both acquires a sense of mastery over a piece of the most modern and powerful technology and establishes an intense contact with some of the deepest ideas from science, from mathematics, and from the art of intellectual model building.

Seymour Papert

Contents

Unit 0: Introduction

I am convinced that the best learning takes place when the learner takes charge [of the learning process]. - Seymour Papert

In this book, in addition to learning a lot of Computer Science concepts, you will do a series of interesting projects and programming activities. You don't need to have any prior programming experience or expertise for this course. This is supposed to be your first encounter with computer programming.

You might ask: Why should I learn CS concepts and Scratch? Why should I bother learning computer programming at all?

The fact is every one of us today works with computers. Your smartphone is a computer which you use for communication and games and so many other things. When you go online to do shopping or to find information you are using computers. When you go to a grocery store the person at the checkout counter is using a computer to scan your items. Your car most likely has a computer to control certain things like the inside temperature.

But, in all these cases we are working with the computer as "consumers" or "users". Someone else – people called "programmers" – at companies such as Microsoft or Google or Cisco created all those services that we use.

I think it is much more exciting to engage with computers as creators, as designers. Can we not ask the computer to do things for us, things which are not already made by someone else? Programming is the new kind of magic that will allow you to be a modern-day wizard. And that is what is meant by "Creative Computing" – designing and creating things using programming.

By the way, there is another great reason to learn computer programming. Practically all future careers will use computers, and so, if you are armed with the power of programming, you will have an edge in your career!

Ok, so, what tool should we use to do creative computing? For this course the tool we are going to use is a language called Scratch. Scratch is an exciting environment in which we can design all kinds of cool stuff – animation, games, interactive art, science experiments, and so on. Scratch is freely available to anyone, and it was developed at MIT.

A few simple guidelines:
As I said earlier, you will do a lot of programming in this course. You will work on a few big projects, and you will also write many small "practice programs".

You will learn and apply concepts of computer programming and computer science when you write these programs. So, work on every program sincerely. Give your best and do not hesitate to ask me questions via email.

Learning programming is just like learning a new sport. The more you practice the better you get at it. Also, you learn when you make mistakes. So, don't feel bad when your programs don't work. In fact, feel happy when they don't work! Because that is how you will learn more.

For this course you should maintain a design notebook. I recommend that you use Microsoft PowerPoint or Word for this purpose. But, if you don't have or know any of these, feel free to use any other word processor or even Notepad. Use the design notebook not only to answer the review questions, but also to make notes of points that you think are important and interesting.

When we write Scratch programs, we use a lot of images and sounds. For your projects, it is certainly ok if you use existing images and sounds. But you will learn a lot more if you try to create these things yourself.

So, use your amazing creativity as much as possible.

All right! We will now open up Scratch and understand its user interface.

Unit 1: First Project in Scratch

*Everybody in this country should learn how to program a computer ...
because it teaches you how to think.* – Steve Jobs

Concepts learnt in this Unit

- Scratch User Interface
- Paint editor
- Sequence
- Motion commands
- Simple looping (repeat, forever)
- Absolute motion
- Relative motion
- Smooth motion using repeat
- Nested looping
- XY geometry
- Costume-based animation
- Multiple backdrops
- 3-D effect using repeat
- Basic sound commands
- Synchronization using broadcasting

Chapter 1.1: First Look at Scratch

Scratch UI:

Start Scratch and get familiar with its basic interface. The following figure points out some of the main parts of the Scratch interface.

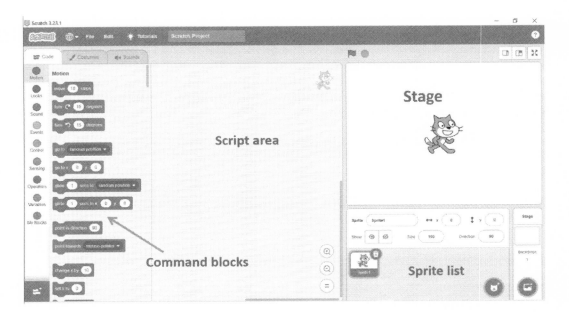

When you start Scratch this is how it looks. It's a bit like a movie maker's studio. You are the movie director and your characters do things according to your instructions.

The white area is called the "stage". That's where all the action happens. Whatever you tell your characters to do they do it on that stage.

Your characters are called "sprites". They are all lined up in the area below the stage.

Now, as you might know, in a movie or a play each character follows a script. Similarly in Scratch every sprite has a script associated with it. You, as the programmer, have to create that script. The "script area" in the above figure is where the sprite's script appears.

The question is how do you build a script? You build a script using the command blocks listed in the middle. There are various types of command blocks: motion, control, sound, etc. You drag and drop these blocks into the script area and connect them together (like jigsaw pieces) to build a script.

Finally, you create, open, or save your Scratch projects by clicking on the File menu.

Sprites:

Every character that will take part in your Scratch project is called a sprite.

Scratch comes with a collection of hundreds of readymade sprites that you can use in your projects. There are animals, people, fantasy characters, cars, planes, and so on. To add a sprite to your project from this Scratch library, click on the appropriate icon.

You can also paint your own sprite by using the built-in paint editor of Scratch. Click on the icon shown above to start the Paint editor and draw your own sprite. If you have used Microsoft Paint or some other similar drawing software, you will find this Scratch Paint Editor very easy to use.

Tip: You can also *modify* an existing sprite using this paint editor.

Stage or background:

Scratch also calls this as "backdrop". Notice the icons below "New backdrop". If you want to change the background, click one of these icons. Scratch itself comes with a lot of interesting backgrounds. If you want to use one of those, click on the "Choose backdrop from library" icon. You will see that there are all kinds of backgrounds: indoor, outdoor, nature, and so on.

If you want to draw your own background, click on the "Paint new backdrop" icon. You will once again see the Paint editor interface.

Tip: You can also *modify* an existing backdrop using this paint editor.

Command blocks and Scripts:

In the left column of the Scratch UI you will see a list of command blocks such as:

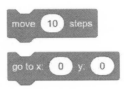

There are several categories (or palettes) of commands, such as "Motion", "Looks", "Sound", and so on. We will learn about these various command blocks throughout this book.

Every sprite has its own program(s) called script(s). You can create a script by snapping together command blocks.

If you want to simply check out what a particular command block does before using it in a script, you can just click on that command block (without dragging it to the script area). For example, we have this command block ⬛. If you click on it the sprite will turn by 15 degrees.

Once you build a script, you can click on it anywhere to run it. For example, this script here asks the sprite to move, take a turn and move again.

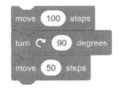

When a script is running, a white border appears around it. That tells us that that script is running. For example, in the script below the sprite turns around itself forever. When we click on it the white border appears around it.

To stop a running script, click on it again. The white border disappears and the script stops running.

Sprite dashboard and tools:

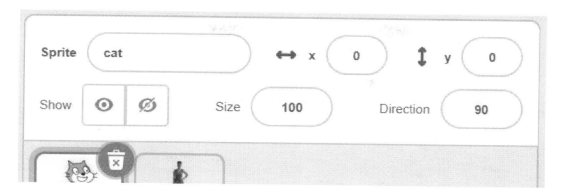

This dashboard shows important information about the selected sprite. In the picture above, we see info about the Scratch cat. The nameplate shows the name of the sprite. The x and y values indicate its location on the screen, the "Show" indicator tells us if it's visible, "Size" indicates its current size, and "Direction" tells us which way it is pointing. You can directly edit any of these boxes to change the sprite's state.

If you right-click a sprite, you get a menu of commands using which you can delete the sprite and create a duplicate (instead of having to add again from the Scratch library).

Review questions:

1. Scratch allows you to use your own image/picture when you draw a new sprite. True or False?

2. What is "Scratch"?
    a. It is a computer programming language
    b. It is a software (like Photoshop) in which you can create graphics and animation
    c. It is a type of computer system like Windows or Linux
    d. It is a collection of readymade animations and video games

3. See the script below:

This script will run when
   a. You click on the Green Flag
   b. You press the ENTER key
   c. You click on the script
   d. You click on the sprite

4. What is the difference between the two following commands?

Programming practice:
Experiment with the following command blocks and create your own scripts.

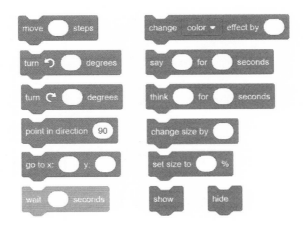

Chapter 1.2: Sequence and Sounds

Build a script as shown below and play with it. Understand the sequence of operations.

Next, build the following script and play with it:

Next, build the following script and run it.

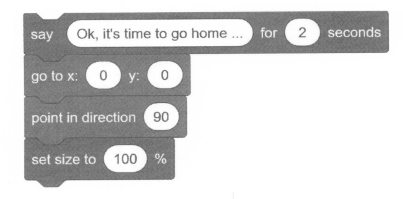

Finally, connect the three scripts all together, and run the whole program together.

Do you have some understanding now of these different command blocks and how scripts are built in Scratch? In this exercise, we learnt the *Sequence* concept as summarized below.

Sequence:
Scratch programs tell the computer precisely what to do, step-by-step. To create a program in Scratch, you need to think about the order of steps. Unlike humans, computer programs do not change the order of the commands given to it.

For example, let's say you were given a "To do" list as follows:
1. Get clothes from the laundry
2. Check mail in the post office box
3. Buy grocery

You may not follow this task-list exactly in the given order. You might go to the grocery shop first, or even skip getting the mail.

Computers do not have this freedom. They would, if given the above list, follow it exactly in the given order, one after the other, making sure every item was completed in a satisfactory manner before going to the next. This concept is called "Sequence" in computer science.

Here is an example of a Scratch script that demonstrates the concept of sequence. The color will change at the very end of the program. The sprite will jump to the center of screen first. And so on.

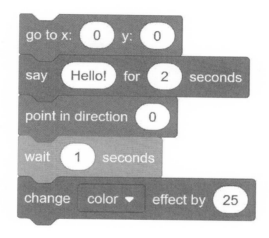

Playing sounds:

One of the exciting features of Scratch is the ability to play sounds.

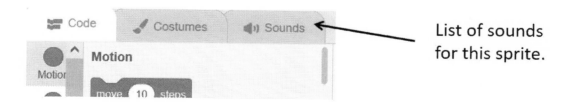

List of sounds for this sprite.

As shown above, every sprite has a tab called "Sounds". Under this tab, you need to collect the sounds that you would like to play in your program. You can import an existing sound from the Scratch library. You can also import your own sound file in MP3 format. If your computer has a sound recording device, you can even record your own voice using the RECORD button.

Once you create a list of sounds for a sprite, you can play these sounds using the following sound commands.

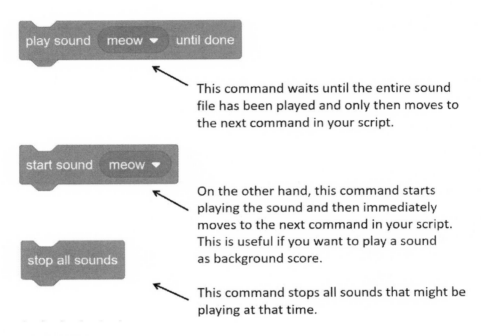

This command waits until the entire sound file has been played and only then moves to the next command in your script.

On the other hand, this command starts playing the sound and then immediately moves to the next command in your script. This is useful if you want to play a sound as background score.

This command stops all sounds that might be playing at that time.

Review questions:

1. How many times will you hear "meow" when you run the script below?

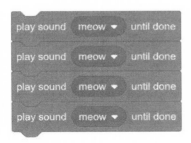

2. How many times will you hear "meow" when you run the script below?

3. We've created the following program for the cat. What will the cat do when we click this script?

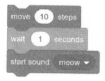

a) It will move, wait for 1 second and then meow.
b) It will move and meow at the same time.
c) It will not do anything.
d) It will meow, wait for 1 second and then move.

Programming practice:

1. Write a script which when clicked does the following. Each action must be visible separately (so you may have to insert the "wait" command).
    - The cat will greet you and tell its name.
    - It will walk 100 steps and then grow double in size.
    - It will slowly move to x = -100, y = -100.
    - It will shrink to original size.
    - It will say "Hey I am down here!"
    - It will bid farewell with a "meow" sound and hide.

2. When clicked your program should play a composition (sequence of notes).

Chapter 1.3: Green flag, Looping, and Costumes

We will now do a programming activity in which there are two sprites. Pick any two sprites from the Scratch library. In my program, I have taken the cat and a space ranger robot.

Create the following scripts for the two sprites:

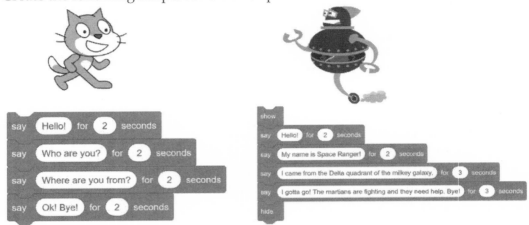

The main problem you will notice is that there is no way to run both these scripts at the same time. You can only click one script at a time.

Green Flag:
This is where the following green flag "hat" block comes in handy.

Just attach this block on top of each of the above scripts as shown below:

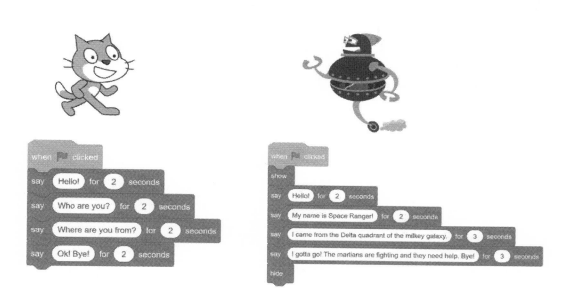

Now, if you click the Green flag at the upper right corner of the Scratch interface (as shown below), you will see that both these scripts start at the same time.

But, things are still not quite right. The two characters speak at the same time, without pausing for each other.

That is a problem with your scripts, not with Scratch. The pauses must be built into the scripts, just like in real life we pause when conversing with someone. See the addition of "wait" commands in the modified scripts below.

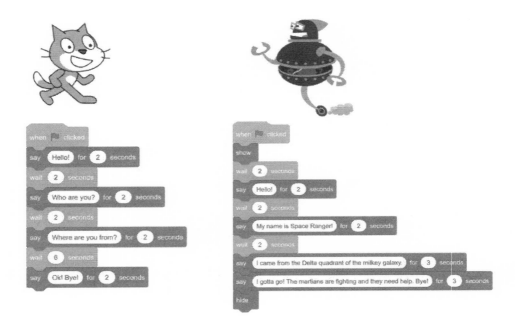

If you click on the Green flag now, you will observe a proper conversation between the two characters.

Next, we will learn the new concept of looping.

Simple looping (repeat, forever):

Looping (also known as *iteration*) is the repetition of a sequence of commands. The "repeat" and "forever" commands in Scratch allow simple looping:

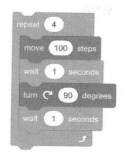

The sprite will move in a square.   The sprite will spin around itself forever.

In order to use looping effectively, it is essential to first get the basic sequence working properly.

For example, let's say we want a sprite to jump up and down repeatedly. We should first get the basic command sequence, i.e. one jump, working properly as shown below:

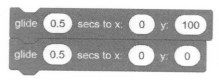

Jumping involves moving up and down. So, just using two different values for "y" should do the trick.

Now, making 4 jumps is a simple matter of putting this sequence inside a REPEAT block:

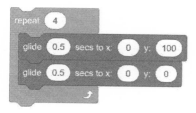

Smooth motion using repeat:

Let's take an example in which we will see an interesting use of REPEAT.

Place your sprite somewhere near the left edge and click the following script.

The sprite will jump to the right by 300 steps. It seems as if the jump was instantaneous. Indeed, most Scratch commands take an extremely short time to run. Looping can, in fact, reveal that these commands are not really instantaneous. Run the following modified script:

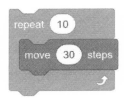

The sprite goes the same distance (10x30 = 300) but a bit more smoothly. That's because the extremely short but finite time taken by "move" adds up 10 times. (Note that the time taken by "move" is the same irrespective of its input, i.e. the # of steps.)

Now, try the following script:

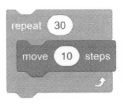

Once again, the sprite goes the same distance (30x10 = 300) but it goes smoothly at a slower speed.

So, there you have it! You can use REPEAT to create smooth motion, and the speed of the motion depends on the size of each step.

The same principle applies to rotation (spinning). The following two scripts spin the sprite but at different speeds.

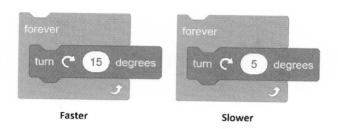

Faster   **Slower**

What if you wanted your sprite to just walk horizontally (east-west) forever? See the following script:

Note the "if on edge, bounce" command. It ensures that the sprite doesn't go past the screen edges. Use the ⬚ command to control the sprite's orientation after bouncing.

Animation using costumes:

Animation, as you know, is an illusion of action or motion. We can make pictures of people, animals, and even of inanimate objects appear alive by making them do things.

Motion is one way to create animation. But, there is one shortcoming in that. Motion commands make the whole sprite move. You cannot move its parts. There is no hand-waving or change of expression or anything like that.

Animation is basically a trick played on our eyes. When we see a succession of slightly changing pictures rapidly one after the other, for example, the pictures of a hand moving up, our eyes think that we actually saw a hand moving up!

In Scratch this series of pictures is called costumes. Every sprite can line up its costumes in the "Costumes" tab. Several Scratch sprites come with costumes of their own. In addition, you can draw costumes using the Paint editor, or you can simply import images from outside. You can also use a camera if your computer has one.

Once you line up the costumes, you use the following commands to actually use these costumes to create animation.

The "next costume" command will make the sprite change its appearance and look like the next costume in its list of costumes. When it reaches the end of the list it goes back to the first costume in the list.

The command "switch to costume" allows the sprite to change to any costume in the list. This is handy when you don't have an orderly series of costumes, but a set of costumes that your sprite wants to use in no particular order.

Let's take an example. For the cat sprite, click on the "Costumes" tab. You will see the following costumes lined up already:

Now, create the following scripts and see what happens when you press the SPACE key again and again
.

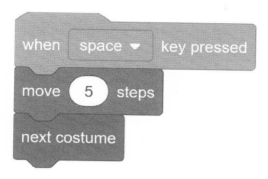

Do you see the cat actually walking (and not just dragging its feet as we saw earlier)?

Can you now make the cat walk back and forth continuously? See the following script:

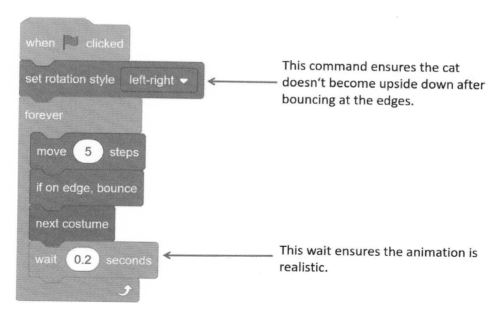

This command ensures the cat doesn't become upside down after bouncing at the edges.

This wait ensures the animation is realistic.

Multiple backdrops:

The Scratch stage can have multiple backdrops. There are a number of ways to create a new backdrop:

- Choose from the Scratch library
- Paint using the paint editor
- Upload an image from your computer
- Take a photo using your camera

Once you have lined up multiple backdrops for the stage, either the stage or any of the sprites can change the backdrop any time using the following command (listed under the "Looks" tab):

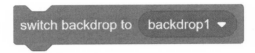

The stage can also use the following command to change backdrops:

Review questions:

1. Let's say you have painted a new penguin sprite. When you run the command "point in direction 90" on the penguin sprite, the penguin looks left instead of right. What is the problem?
    a. Direction 90 means the left direction
    b. You painted the original image of the penguin to look left
    c. There is a bug in the script
    d. The center of the sprite is not correct

2. What is the distance covered in the script shown below?

a. 5 steps
b. 20 steps
c. 25 steps
d. 100 steps

3. To make your animation look realistic you should have as many costumes as possible. True or False?

Programming practice:

1. From the Scratch library load a sprite that has flying costumes (e.g. bat or parrot). Write a script to make the sprite change costume each time the space bar is pressed. Add code so that the sprite will face to the left, move a few steps and also change costume when the left arrow key is pressed. So, it should look as if the sprite is flying west each time you press left arrow key.

2. You can make the Scratch cat walk by using the "next costume" command as shown below. Do the same using the "switch to costume" command.

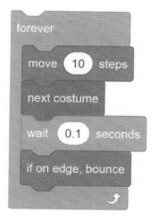

3. Use existing costumes (in the Scratch library) to create animation, such as, a walking boy or a fire-breathing dragon.

4. Draw your own costumes using the Paint editor.

Chapter 1.4: XY Geometry and Nested Looping

Using the motion commands in Scratch you can create all kinds of interesting motion. First let us understand the layout of the Scratch stage and how several motion commands make use of it.

XY Geometry:

We use the screen in Scratch as a geometric plane. Every point on the screen has X and Y coordinates. You might have learnt about this in your school mathematics.

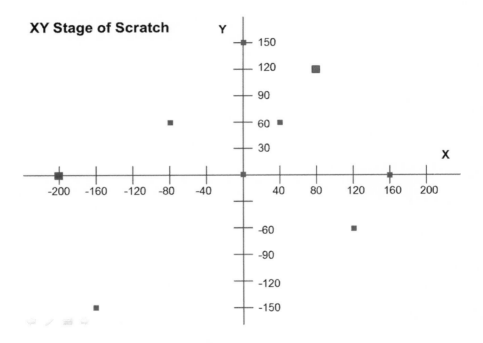

Every point on the screen has two coordinates: x and y. Imagine two number lines laid out on the screen: one horizontally and the other vertically, both intersecting at 0. The horizontal line is called the X axis, and the vertical line is called the Y axis. The distance of a point from the Y axis is called the X coordinate, and the distance from the X axis is called the Y coordinate.

For example, for the blue point here its distance from the Y axis is 80, so its X coordinate is 80. And its distance from the X axis is 120, so its Y coordinate is 120.

For the dark red point its distance from the Y axis is -200, so its X value is -200. And its distance from the X axis is 0, so its Y coordinate is 0.

Every sprite in Scratch has a center point which you can view (and change) in the Paint editor. The X Y coordinates of this center point are assumed to be the X Y coordinates of the sprite. When the sprite moves these values also change automatically.

Now that we understand what X Y coordinates are let us look at a few Scratch commands that make use of these coordinates.

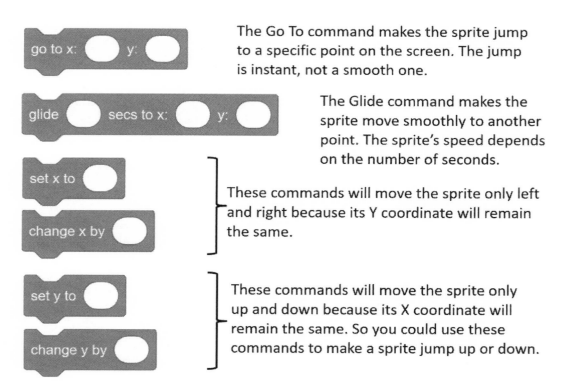

The Go To command makes the sprite jump to a specific point on the screen. The jump is instant, not a smooth one.

The Glide command makes the sprite move smoothly to another point. The sprite's speed depends on the number of seconds.

These commands will move the sprite only left and right because its Y coordinate will remain the same.

These commands will move the sprite only up and down because its X coordinate will remain the same. So you could use these commands to make a sprite jump up or down.

The SET commands are interesting because they move the sprite to a specific point no matter where the sprite is right now. Whereas, the CHANGE command depends on the sprite's current location.

For example, if you say "CHANGE X by 10" the sprite will move to its right by 10 pixels. If you run "CHANGE X by 10" once more, the sprite will again move to its right by 10 pixels.

But, if you say "SET X to 100", the sprite will jump to where X is 100. And if you run "SET X to 100" once more, nothing will happen because the sprite is already at X = 100.

There is one important thing to note about all these commands shown here. The orientation, or, the direction in which the sprite is facing, does not change when you use any of these commands.

Orientation of a sprite is basically the direction in which it is facing. It is shown in terms of the angle made with the North direction. So if a sprite is facing North its direction value is 0.

Initially all sprites are facing east, which means their direction is 90. You can change a sprite's orientation using one of the commands shown below.

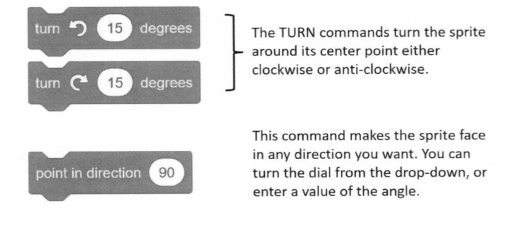

The TURN commands turn the sprite around its center point either clockwise or anti-clockwise.

This command makes the sprite face in any direction you want. You can turn the dial from the drop-down, or enter a value of the angle.

Nested looping:

Nesting means having one loop inside another. See the example below:

The following script makes the sprite jump up and down. Repeat makes the jump appear smooth.

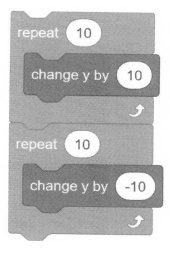

What if we wanted the sprite to jump 5 times?

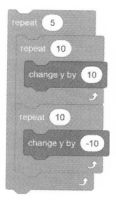

The two inside repeat loops together make the sprite jump once, and the outside loop makes the jump happen 5 times. Thus, nesting of loops can open up interesting opportunities.

Review questions:

1. A sprite has a script as shown below:

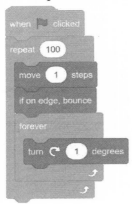

When you click on the Green flag:

a. The sprite will move 100 steps
b. The sprite will move forever
c. The sprite will move 1 step
d. The sprite will move 100 steps and
   turn 100 degrees

2. As a sprite moves up, its X-value ...
    a. Gets bigger
    b. Get smaller
    c. Stays the same

3. How do you make a sprite jump up and down?
    a. Use a pair of "Glide" commands
    b. Use a pair of "go to x, y" commands
    c. Use the "change y" command in a pair of Repeat blocks
    d. All of the above

Programming practice:

Note: Look up http://abhayjoshi.net/scratch/book0/videos.htm to check out videos of sample solutions.

1. Write a "commotion" program in which various animals are made to perform different actions, such as:
    o constantly jumping up and down
    o spinning around itself
    o roaming around the screen
    o etc.

Chapter 1.5: Animation Mini-project

This is a mini-project assignment for you, in which you will apply all the concepts and commands learnt so far. The specification of this project is as follows:

Specification: About-me or Monologue

In this project you have two options: (1) Make a story of yourself (and your friends and family) or (2) Design a monologue.

- **About-me**: One primary sprite (for you) and other sprites (friends and family). In the animation you (i.e. the sprite representing you) talk about yourself – your name, family, house, hobbies, etc. Other sprites don't say anything or perform any actions.
- **Monologue**: Similar to "about-me" except the sprite will make up its own story.

Project Requirements:

- Green flag should start the animation.
- Only 1 active sprite.
- Use as many commands learnt so far as possible (movement, rotation, etc.).
- Use sounds and costumes.

Note: Look up http://abhayjoshi.net/scratch/book0/videos.htm to check out videos of sample solutions.

Chapter 1.6: More Motion and Broadcasting

Absolute motion:

Absolute motion refers to motion whose result *does not* depend on your current position and direction. For example, "Going to Washington DC" is absolute motion because you will end up in Washington DC no matter where you currently are.

The following Scratch commands (among others) describe absolute motion because the resulting position or direction *does not* depend on the sprite's previous position or direction.

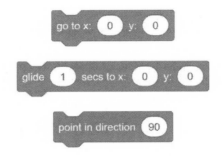

Relative motion:

In contrast to absolute motion, relative motion depends on your current position and direction. For example, "Turn right" is relative motion because the resulting direction depends on your current direction.

The following example Scratch commands describe relative motion because the resulting position or direction *does* depend on the sprite's previous position or direction.

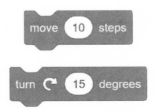

3-D effect using looping:

Everything in Scratch – sprites and backgrounds – is 2-D (two dimensional). You can't make a sprite turn around and face away from you (unless of course you have a suitable costume). But there is a bit of 3-D that you can achieve with the use of repetition and change of size. When a sprite moves away from you, its size shrinks. Conversely, if you decrease its size it will appear as if it is moving away. The same principle applies to growing and increasing the size.

Load the costumes "Dove 1" and "Dove 2" and load any outdoor background. Create and run the following script. Do you see a bird flying towards you?

Synchronization using broadcasting:

When you write a program that contains multiple sprites that interact with each other in some way, you need to worry about synchronization – which basically means proper coordination of their actions.

To understand synchronization, let us look at an example, as shown above. Here, we have two sprites – Gobo and cat – talking with each other. If you run the program what will happen? They both will talk at the same time! There will be no proper sequence or coordination. That's not what you expect, right? To make it a proper dialog, the Gobo should say "Hi" first, then, the cat should reply by saying "Hello", and so on.

So we say that there is no *synchronization* in this program. Do you now see the meaning of synchronization?

You might have heard the word "Broadcasting" in the context of radio and TV. When you tune into a radio station, you are actually listening to something that was broadcast from a radio station.

Broadcasting basically means sending a message to anyone who cares to listen. So, when someone gives a public speech, he/she is giving a *broadcast* speech.

In Scratch, broadcasting has a similar meaning. When you use the BROADCAST command (under the "Events" tab), your sprite sends a message that goes to every sprite in your program and even to the stage.

But, just like not everyone is interested in listening to the radio, not every sprite may be interested in hearing the message. So, if a sprite is interested in receiving that message it uses the command WHEN I RECEIVE. So, in effect, broadcasting can also be used to pass messages one-to-one, i.e. between two entities.

So here are all the commands related to broadcasting:

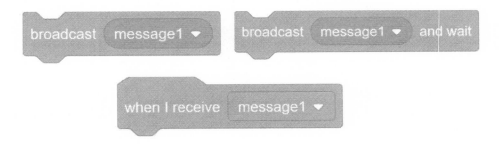

WHEN I RECEIVE is an event and works just like WHEN GREEN FLAG CLICKED. When the message is received the script underneath that event runs.

Every time the exact same message is received the script runs again.

There are two flavors of the BROADCAST command as shown above.

In the first flavor, the sending sprite sends the broadcast message and immediately goes to the next command in the script, if there is any.

But, in the second flavor, the sending sprite sends the broadcast message and waits – until all listening sprites have received the message and completely run each of their "WHEN I RECEIVE" scripts.

Example:

To understand the difference between these two broadcasts, run the following experiment.

Take any two sprites sprite1 and sprite2. Create the following script for sprite1:

Create the following script for sprite2:

And now run the program by clicking on Green Flag. Observe the conversation. You will notice that it doesn't look right. Now, replace the "broadcast" command in sprite1's script by "broadcast and wait". Run the program again by clicking the Green Flag.

Review questions:

1. The Scratch command "point in direction" causes relative motion. True or False?

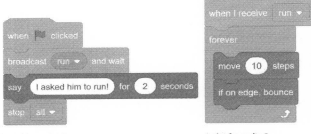

2. If you run the _____ command, the new position of the sprite on the screen depends on the current position.
   a) True
   b) False

3. We have two sprites sprite1 and sprite2. They have scripts as shown below:

Script for sprite 1	Script for sprite 2

What will happen when the green flag is clicked?
   a) Sprite1 will say "I asked him to run".
   b) Sprite2 will stop running after 2 seconds because the STOP command will stop the program after 2 seconds.
   c) Sprite1 will never say anything.
   d) The results will be unpredictable.

4. In a particular game program, sprite1 is supposed to send a "GO" signal to all sprites so that they can start doing their work, and then sprite1 is supposed to count time. Which of the following commands should sprite1 use to send the "GO" signal?

B1:   B2:
   a) Sprite1 should use command B1
   b) Sprite1 should use command B2

c) Sprite1 should first use B1 and then B2

d) Sprite1 should first use B2 and then B1

5. Let's say we have two sprites Kitty and Abby. Their respective scripts are shown below.

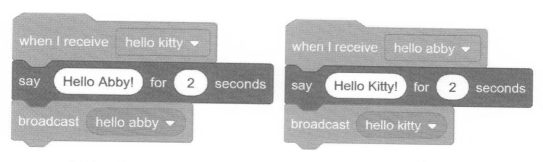

Script for Kitty   **Script for Abby**

What will happen if you click on one of these scripts?

   a. Nothing happens - this doesn't work because there is a loop.
   b. Kitty and Abby will keep saying "Hello" to each other until you hit the red stop button.
   c. Kitty and Abby will say "Hello" to each other only once.
   d. Kitty and Abby will say "Hello" to each other simultaneously.

Programming practice:

Note: Look up http://abhayjoshi.net/scratch/book0/videos.htm to check out videos of sample solutions.

1. Write a "circus" program in which the ringmaster calls animals/actors one by one and each performs some act.

2. Write a "roll call" program in which the teacher calls students one by one and each says "present" if present. Show one or two as being absent – someone else will inform the teacher.

Chapter 1.7: Project Animation

This is a project assignment for you, in which you will apply all the concepts and commands learnt so far. The specification of this project is as follows:

Specification: Short story

In this project you will design a short story animation. This can be a nursery rhyme, a folk story, or a clip from your favorite story. The story should be narrated as sub-titles or as part of the animation.

Project Requirements:
- Green flag should start the animation.
- At least 2 sprites.
- Draw at least one background.
- Use as many commands learnt so far as possible (movement, rotation, broadcasting, etc.).
- Use sounds and costumes.
- Sprite names must be as per the story, and not sprite1, sprite2, etc.
- As each line of the story appears on the screen (anywhere) animation of that line should be visible.
- Story should be slow and easy to understand.
- It should take at least 10 seconds but not more than a minute.

Note: Look up http://abhayjoshi.net/scratch/book0/videos.htm to check out videos of sample solutions.

Write in your Design book:
- A short description of your project
- Answer these questions:
  1. What did you learn?
  2. What was exciting?
  3. What was challenging?

Unit 2: Interactive Animation

Young people today need to be able to use their learning muscles to innovate and create, and ultimately to adapt and transform themselves several times over in one lifetime. – James Paul Gee

Concepts learnt in this Unit

- Events
- Reset script
- Graphic effects
- Concurrency
- User interaction using keyboard
- Conditions: YES/NO questions
- Sensing touch
- Conditionals (IF)
- Conditionals (IF-Else)
- Stopping scripts

Chapter 2.1: Events, Reset Scripts, Concurrency

While working on your first project (of the previous unit) you might have noticed one problem. At the end of the program, you have to manually bring all sprites back to where they are supposed to be at the beginning and change their appearance back to what it was. Otherwise, the next time you run the program, it doesn't work properly. To avoid this manual work, you can make use of an idea called "Reset script".

But, before we understand how to write reset scripts, let's understand the concept of events.

Events:

Events are outside happenings that create some sort of a signal. For example, the "ringing of a phone" is an event that tells us that someone is calling. "Traffic light turning red" is an event that signals that cars need to stop. Real world is full of events. Following are some of the commonly used events in Scratch:

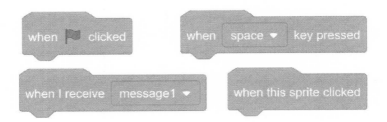

Every sprite in your program will have scripts to respond to the events that that sprite is interested in. For example, the paddle sprite in a game might respond to the "when up arrow key pressed" event by moving up a little as shown below:

Reset script:

Every sprite has a set of attributes (properties). We can call this set its "state".
- Position on the screen (X, Y)
- Orientation (Angle with North)
- Color (default value is 0)
- Size (default is 100%)
- Visibility (visible or invisible)
- Costume
- Graphic effects

After we run scripts, one or more of these properties change. For example, see this script.

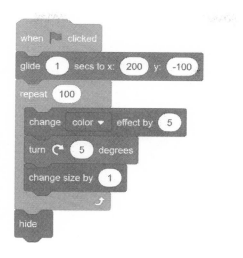

After running it, the sprite's location, direction, color, size, and visibility will all have changed. We need to reset these back to the original values before we run this program again. This is done by the following script:

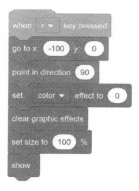

This is called a "reset script". By simply pressing the "r" key (or whichever key you use in your script) you can set the sprite properties to their original values.

Concurrency - running scripts in parallel:

We will try to understand the concept of concurrency through some examples. Start with a program in which a sprite wants to move and talk at the same time. Can a single script do it? Try the following script in which we wish to have the sprite say hello while walking back and forth.

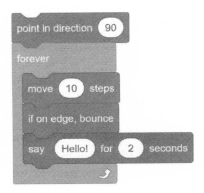

It doesn't quite work as expected, does it? This is where concurrency comes to help. Split this script into two scripts as shown below:

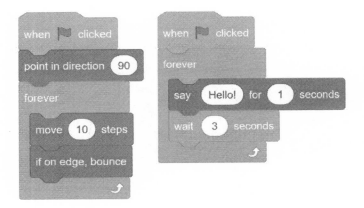

Now if you click on the Green flag, the sprite will continue moving non-stop and say hello every 3 seconds.

Concurrency basically means doing multiple actions at the same time. People like you and me are doing multiple things at the same time, all the time! For example, when we take a walk, we listen to music or talk on the phone, watch for road signs, react to a buzzing fly, and so on. All these actions happen concurrently.

Here is another Scratch example:

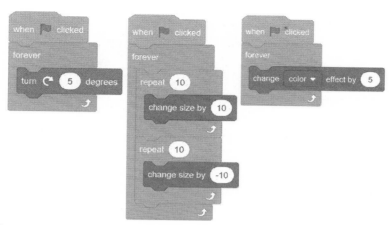

We have three scripts for the same sprite. The first script makes the sprite spin around itself. The second script changes its size continuously. And the third script changes its color continuously.

Because all three scripts start with the same signal, which is "Green Flag clicked", the sprite will appear as if it is performing these actions at the same time, that is, concurrently.

Review questions:

1. A sprite has a script as shown below.

If you make a duplicate of this script and click on the green flag again, what will happen?

a. The sprite will run twice as fast since both scripts run at the same time.
b. Nothing will happen because there is an error.
c. Only one script will run because the two scripts are identical
d. The sprite will not run in a straight line.

2. It is a good idea to write a separate RESET script which:
   a. Restarts Scratch and opens your project file again
   b. Takes the sprite to its original position and direction
   c. Hides the sprite when the program is over
   d. Makes the sprite look in the East direction

3. See the following two scripts written for the Cat:

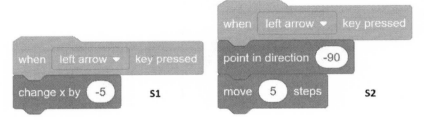

Which of the following statements is true?
   a) The two scripts will do the exact same thing.
   b) The script S1 will move the Cat to the right.
   c) In script S1 the Cat moves left, but keeps facing right.
   d) In script S2 the Cat moves left, but keeps facing right.

Programming practice:

Note: Look up http://abhayjoshi.net/scratch/book0/videos.htm to check out videos of sample solutions.

1. Make a bird sprite fly around the screen while changing size and color at the same time. Also have it make some sound every 5 seconds.

2. Make a ball roll from left to right of the screen. The ball appears at the left edge, rolls to the right, disappears across the right edge, and reappears again at the left edge.

Graphic Effects:

Scratch provides a bunch of interesting graphic effects that you can use to make your animation very exciting. They are available under the "Looks" tab.

Color effect:

At the top of the list is color. Changing colors is of course very exciting, isn't it! The SET command simply sets the color to a specific value. There are about 200 different values you can use – from 0 to 200. The "CHANGE" command adds a number to your current color value. Why don't you experiment with these values and discover which value gives you which color?

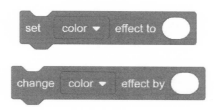

This example script will show you 10 different colors in the range 0 to 200.

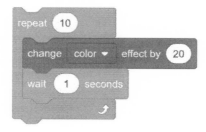

Ghost Effect:

Ghost effect has to do with disappearing slowly. So every time you increase the ghost value, the sprite will become fainter and fainter. At the value of 100 it will disappear completely.

If you want to make the sprite appear again, reduce value gradually back to 0.

This example script makes a sprite disappear and reappear – just like a ghost.

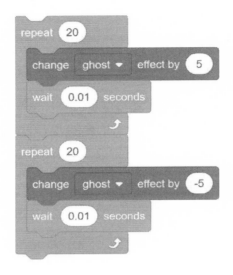

Fisheye Effect:

Fisheye effect is like pumping air into a balloon. Except in this case you pump air into your sprite. Just like the balloon bulges slowly as the air is pumped into it, your Sprite will bulge as you increase the FISHEYE value. There is no limit to how much air you can pump into your sprite.

To deflate, that is, to take the air out again, decrease the FISHEYE value gradually.

You can use a pair of repeat loops (as shown in the "ghost" effect above) to inflate a sprite and deflate it back to normal.

Whirl Effect:

WHIRL effect is about stirring your sprite with a stirrer as if it were a liquid. Think of your washing machine in which you wash clothes. The machine twists and turns the clothes, right?

Similarly, the WHIRL effect twists your sprite in either direction – right or left – depending on whether you increase the WHIRL value or decrease it.

You can use a bunch of repeat loops (as shown in the "ghost" effect above) to gradually twist a sprite clockwise and then twist it anticlockwise and then bring it back to normal.

Pixelate Effect:

Pixelate effect allows you to zoom into your sprite making it more grainy. You might have seen this type of effect in some of the older video games.

The maximum you can pixelate, that is, blur the sprite completely, is about 500. Beyond that the sprite becomes invisible. To bring it back to normal, reduce the PIXELATE value.

You can use a pair of repeat loops (as shown in the "ghost" effect above) to gradually zoom into a sprite and zoom back out.

How to clear effects:

For any of these graphical effects that we saw so far, there are 2 simple ways to cancel the effect, and bring your sprite back to its normal appearance. The

CLEAR GRAPHIC EFFECTS command cancels all graphical effects. If you want to just cancel one of the effects, use the SET command and set the value to 0.

Review questions:

4. Your sprite has undergone a lot of color change in your animation. So, in your reset script you would like to restore the sprite back to its original color. Which command will you use?

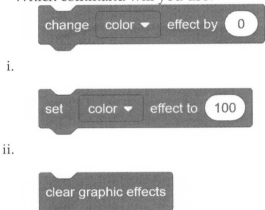

i.

ii.

iii.

   a) i only
   b) ii only
   c) iii only
   d) i or iii
   e) ii or iii

Programming practice:

3. Insert graphic effects in your earlier animation program or in a new animation.

Chapter 2.2: Keyboard Interaction and Conditionals

User interaction using keyboard:

One of the most interesting features of Scratch is that it allows the user to interact with programs. Your programs need not be just animations that one has to watch, but, they can be interactive.

Scratch provides an event block called   . If you write a script under this event, it will run every time the user presses the specified key.

See these examples. In game programs arrow keys are typically used to move sprites. Here, the UP ARROW key runs a script in which the sprite moves 10 steps upwards.

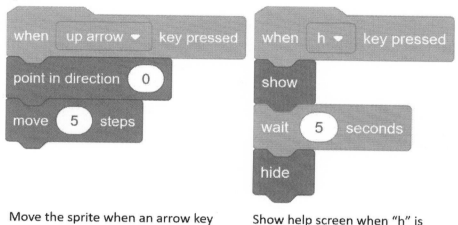

Move the sprite when an arrow key is pressed.

Show help screen when "h" is pressed.

In the second example, the h key makes the sprite visible for a short time – this sprite could possibly be a "HELP" screen which pops up for a short time and then goes away.

Sensing touch:

In Scratch, you can check if things are touching each other, and use that information in the conditional statements (such as IF, Wait until, Repeat until, etc.) which we will learn shortly. Here are the sensing conditions:

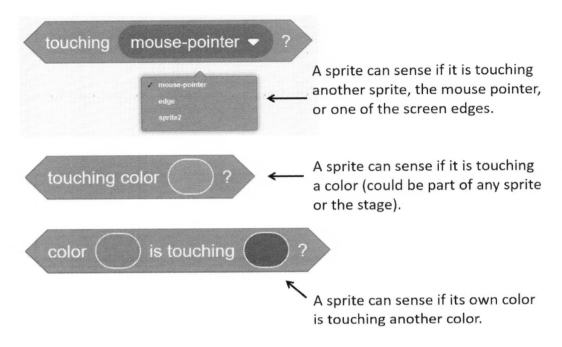

A sprite can sense if it is touching another sprite, the mouse pointer, or one of the screen edges.

A sprite can sense if it is touching a color (could be part of any sprite or the stage).

A sprite can sense if its own color is touching another color.

An example of how sensing can be used in a conditional statement:

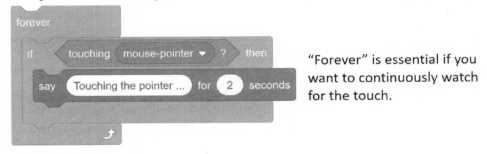

"Forever" is essential if you want to continuously watch for the touch.

See below to learn the IF command.

Conditional statements (IF):

In Computer Science there is a special type of question called the TRUE-FALSE question. For this type of question the answer can only be either TRUE or FALSE. For example, "Is it raining?" Or, "Are you going home?" Or, "Is 25 a square of 5?" The answer to all these questions is either TRUE or FALSE. There is no other possible answer.

These questions are known as CONDITIONS.

Scratch provides many such conditional questions and they are shown as diamond blocks. If you look under the SENSING and OPERATORS tabs, you will see several conditions. Here are some examples:

TOUCHING is a condition which basically is the question "Am I touching so and so?" There is another diamond block called TOUCHING COLOR which is the question "Am I touching this color?" Under OPERATORS there are diamond blocks that compare numbers.

Now, in real life, we use the TRUE-FALSE questions to take some action. For example, if the answer to the question "Is it raining?" is TRUE (or YES), we might decide to take the umbrella to school.

Similarly, in Scratch we have a command called IF that we can use if a condition is TRUE. In the example shown below, if the sprite is TOUCHING another sprite called "fire", the sprite will say "Help! Help!" and then back off by 100 steps.

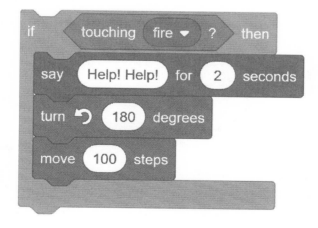

Conditional statements (IF-Else):

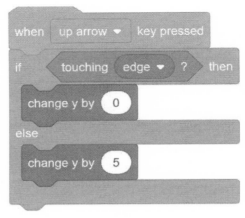

This is a variation of the IF command described above. See this example:

We want to move the sprite upward but not take it beyond the top edge. The condition in the above command is: "Is the sprite touching the edge?" If the answer is YES, the sprite doesn't move. If the answer is NO, the sprite moves up 5 steps.

So, the IF-Else command offers a fork in the process of decision-making.

Review questions:

1. See the following script:

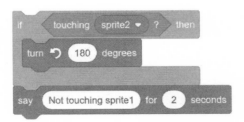

Which of the following statements is true?
   a) The SAY command will never run.
   b) The SAY command will run only if this sprite is not touching sprite1.
   c) The SAY command will run even if this sprite is touching sprite1.
   d) The SAY command will run only if this sprite is touching sprite1.

2. What will happen if we run the following script?

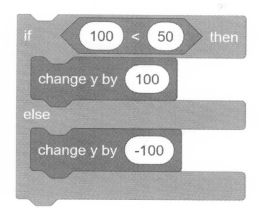

   a. The sprite will move up
   b. The sprite will move down

3. What will happen if you run the following script?

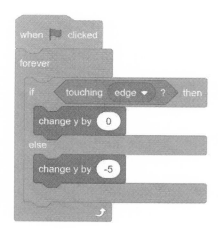

   a. The sprite will not move.
   b. The sprite will rise up and stop when it hits the top edge.
   c. The sprite will fall down and stop when it hits the bottom edge.
   d. The sprite will jump up and down continuously.

4. Are the following two scripts equivalent?

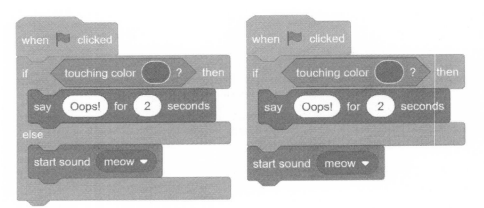

    a) Yes
    b) No

5. See the following two scripts S1 and S2.

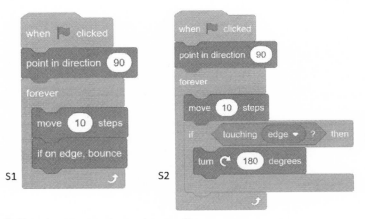

Which of the following statements is true?

    a) These two scripts do the exact same thing.
    b) In script S1 the sprite bounces only on the left and right edges of the screen.

c) In script S2 bouncing also happens if the sprite touches any other sprite.

d) The scripts S1 and S2 will behave differently.

Programming practice:

Note: Look up http://abhayjoshi.net/scratch/book0/videos.htm to check out videos of sample solutions.

1. Design a program in which a ball bounces up and down and is deflected by a paddle. The user should be able to move the paddle horizontally using the arrow keys.

2. Design a program in which there are several separate color circles (red, blue, green, etc.) on the screen. When the green flag is clicked an animal sprite starts moving around the screen and whenever it touches a circle its color becomes the same as the circle's. (Tips: (1) Consider using costumes for the animal. (2) (Optional) To make the animal sprite follow the pointer, consider using the "point towards" and "move" commands in a forever loop.)

Stopping scripts:

The STOP commands (under the "Control" tab) allow us to stop Scratch scripts in various ways.

The "STOP all" command stops all active scripts in your Scratch project. For example, the script below checks if the allotted time has been used up, and if so, it stops the game. (Note: "time" is called a *variable*; we will learn about variables later in this book.)

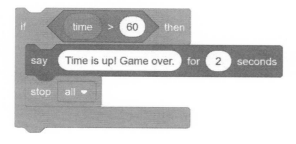

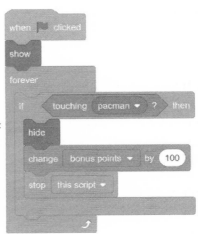

The command "STOP this script" stops only the current script. In the adjoining script, a "prize" sprite waits until it touches "pacman". Since it has nothing else to do afterwards, it hides and stops its script.

Finally, the command "STOP other scripts in sprite" is useful when you want to only stop scripts of the current sprite. If you want to stop all scripts of the current sprite you would need to do as shown in the following hypothetical script:

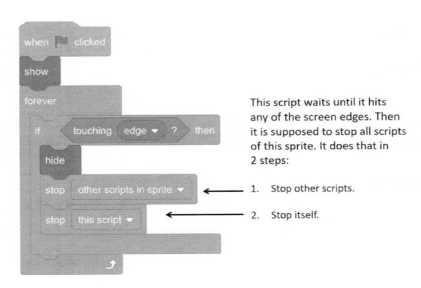

This script waits until it hits any of the screen edges. Then it is supposed to stop all scripts of this sprite. It does that in 2 steps:

1. Stop other scripts.

2. Stop itself.

With the help of all the concepts learnt so far, we are now ready to take up a game project. Let's go for it!

Chapter 2.3: Project Helicopter

Description:
Using arrow keys fly a helicopter. Show the effect of gravity, i.e. if you don't do anything, the helicopter should automatically move down slowly. So, "Down" arrow key is not needed. The helicopter should be able to land on a helipad. Show moving clouds (just for fun). Have some indication, such as blinking lights or spinning fans, to indicate that the Helicopter engine is running.

Concepts used:
- User interaction (keyboard)
- Costumes
- IF-ELSE and sensing touch

Sprites:
1. Helicopter
2. Landing pad (can also be part of the stage)
3. Clouds

User Interaction:
- Green flag resets everything and starts the helicopter engine.
- SPACE BAR adds effect of gravity
- Arrow keys (except "down") control the helicopter

Additional requirements:
- The helicopter should land only if its landing gear touches the helipad.

The following image shows one possible implementation of this game.

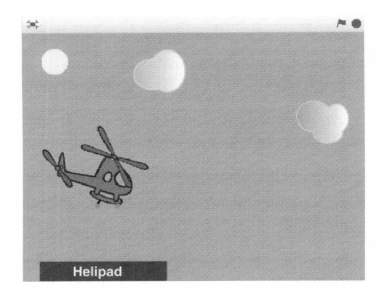

Note: Look up http://abhayjoshi.net/scratch/book0/videos.htm to check out videos of sample solutions.

Write in your Design book:
- A short description of your project
- Answer these questions:
  1. What did you learn?
  2. What was exciting?
  3. What was challenging?

Unit 3: First Game Project

It's not what you know about the computer that's important,
but your ability to do things with it. – Seymour Papert

Concepts learnt in this Unit

- User interaction using mouse pointer
- Conditionals (Wait until)
- Variables – numbers
- Variables as sliders
- Keyboard events (polling)
- User input (buttons)

Chapter 3.1: Mouse Interaction

User interaction using mouse pointer:

Here are the mouse event blocks that Scratch provides. You are already quite familiar with the event WHEN GREEN FLAG CLICKED.

The other event is called WHEN THIS SPRITE CLICKED which invokes a script when you click on that particular sprite. Imagine a button sprite, for example, that you could activate through such a script.

In the script shown below, if you click on the bird sprite, the bird makes a "bird" sound and says "Chirp chirp".

There is a similar event for the stage also:

Another interesting thing you can do in Scratch is that you can make a sprite follow the mouse pointer. The script shown below explains how this can be done. You make the sprite point towards the pointer and then take a small step.

If this is done continuously, the effect is to make the sprite follow the mouse pointer.

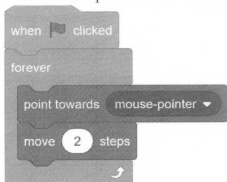

In fact, the same idea can be used to make one sprite follow another. In the script below a "baby" sprite follows its "mother" everywhere she goes!

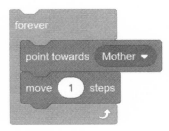

User input (buttons):

It is common to have pushbuttons (or rather click-buttons) to allow users to interact with programs. See the examples below:

A click-button has the following properties:
- It is usually rectangular, oval, or circular.
- It has a label that describes what action it initiates.
- When you click on it, the specified action is performed.

To implement a click-button:
- Get a button sprite (you can use the built-in sprites or draw your own)
- Label it appropriately
- Use a "When sprite clicked" event to make the button active
- Send a broadcast message to whoever is supposed to carry out that action

Here is an example script for a "Draw" button:

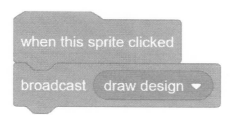

When clicked, the button sprite sends a broadcast message to let everyone know that it was clicked. The actual drawing would be drawn by some other sprite when it receives this message. (In case you are wondering, you can draw all kinds of designs in Scratch – we will learn all about it later in "Pen art".)

Review questions:

1. We have the following script written for the Cat sprite.

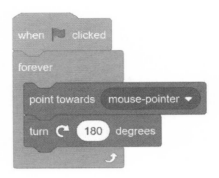

What will happen when we click on the Green flag?

   a) The Cat will follow the mouse pointer all the time.
   b) The Cat will point away from the mouse pointer all the time.
   c) The Cat will point towards the mouse pointer all the time.
   d) The Cat will move away from the mouse pointer all the time.

Programming practice:

Note: Look up http://abhayjoshi.net/scratch/book0/videos.htm to check out videos of sample solutions.

1. Write a program in which the sprite jumps to the pointer whenever you click anywhere on the stage.

2. Write a program in which the sprite doesn't allow the mouse pointer to touch it. It runs away as soon as you move the pointer to it. The sprite stays inside the visible screen.

3. Write a program in which a wizard performs various types of magic for his audience. Provide a button for each magic, such that when you click on it, that particular magic is performed. For example, a button called "Frog" will turn a boy into a frog temporarily and then back to human form.

Chapter 3.2: Variables

Variables – numbers:

As you might know already, computers have a *temporary* memory called RAM. They use this memory to store information and do their work. For example, when you use a calculator program to make calculations, the computer stores the numbers you type in its memory. This memory is called "temporary memory" because the information goes away if you shut down the computer.

How does your program make use of this memory? That's where *variables* come in the picture. A *variable* is a location in this temporary memory, and each variable has a name. In Scratch, you can create a variable by clicking on the button "Make a variable" under the "Data" tab. Once you create a variable it becomes available to your program to store information.

When you no longer need a variable, you can delete it by right-clicking on the variable name and selecting "delete variable".

The word "variable" means something that can vary or change, and indeed variables can contain any value. Scratch provides commands that you can use in your scripts to store information in variables and then change it later.

The SET command stores a value in a variable. The value can be any number – negative or positive, whole, or decimal.

Later, you can change the value by using the command CHANGE. The CHANGE command adds the given number to the variable.

Let's look at an example of how variables can be used. Here we have a script for the game of maze. We have a variable called "Bonus points". In this script, this variable is incremented by 10 when a prize sprite touches the pacman.

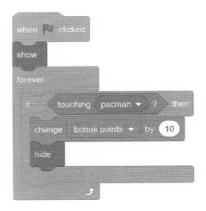

Important: Always initialize number variables to some value (such as 0) at the beginning of the program.

Variables as sliders:

Let's use an example to understand this concept. Let's say we have defined a new variable called "speed". After creating the variable, it will show up on the screen as below:

If you right-click on this, you will see an option called "slider". Select this option. Now the variable will look like this:

It has become a slider variable. The user can drag the white knob and change the value of "speed" even while the program is running.

You (the programmer) can set lower and upper limits on this slider variable. Just right click once again and choose "set slider min and max". For example, if you entered min=10 and max=40 the slider will only allow values in this range.

Review questions:

1. For which of the following cases would we need to use a variable?
   a) We want to make the cat move forever, without ever stopping.
   b) We want to switch to the next costume when the spacebar is pressed.
   c) We want to keep track of the score in a game.
   d) For all of the above.

2. What is the value of "score" after we run this script?

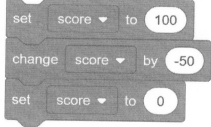

   a) 100
   b) 50
   c) 150
   d) 0

Programming practice:

Note: Look up http://abhayjoshi.net/scratch/book0/videos.htm to check out videos of sample solutions.

1. Write a program in which the sprite counts 1, 2, 3, ... infinity!

Chapter 3.3: Project Game of Maze

Before we look at the specification of this game, let's learn a couple of new ideas which would be useful in this project.

The "Wait until" command:

As we saw earlier, *conditions* are questions that only require a binary answer (yes/no, true/false). You are already familiar with how to use conditions in the IF command.

Sometimes in our programs, we want a sprite to just wait for some condition to become true.

For example, here is a program in which a "prize" sprite is just sitting to be eaten by the *pacman* sprite. When *pacman* touches the prize, it is supposed to disappear.

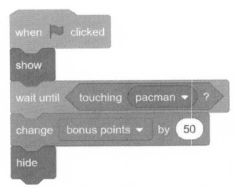

WAIT UNTIL simply waits as long as the CONDITION is false. As soon as the condition becomes true, it stops waiting and the script moves to the next command.

Keyboard events (polling):

There are two ways to get keyboard input: one is using events (known in CS as "interrupt driven"), which we have already seen. The following is an event that signals a key-press and immediately runs the script. This script is called an "event handler".

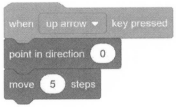

The other way is called "polling" in which the program actively checks if a particular key is pressed.

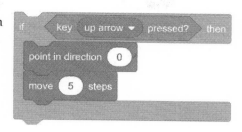

If you want to check this continuously you must use a forever loop:

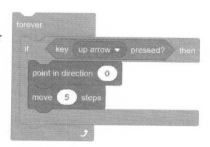

Polling (in a Forever loop) runs continuously taking CPU time, whereas event handlers do not take CPU time, because they sleep and are "woken up" when the event occurs. But, precisely for that reason, a tight loop like the one above is more responsive to user actions than the event-based approach. Another advantage of polling is that the program has full control on when to handle keyboard signals. When the program stops, polling also stops, whereas event handlers would run even if the program has stopped.

Another interesting advantage of polling is that you can combine multiple events using logic operators as shown below:

Maze Project Specification:
- Help an object, such as a pacman, travel thru a maze to reach a target.
- Sprite names must not be sprite1, sprite2, etc.
- Use the "h" key to show help, "Green flag" to set things up, and "Space bar" to start the game.
- Basic features:
  - A simple maze

- o Clearly visible "Start" and "Finish" locations
- o Prizes to eat along the way
- o Pacman moves with arrow keys or follows the pointer
- o Touching the walls of the maze makes pacman go back to Start
- Additional features:
  - o Moving (or spinning) obstacles, when touched pacman resets (goes back to Start)
  - o A monster follows pacman forever; when touched pacman resets
  - o Use a variable to track prize points and penalties.
  - o Timer

The following image shows one example implementation of this game.

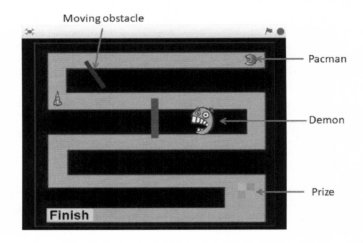

Note: Look up http://abhayjoshi.net/scratch/book0/videos.htm to check out videos of sample solutions.

Write in your Design book:
- A short description of your project
- Answer these questions:
  1. What did you learn?
  2. What was exciting?
  3. What was challenging?

Unit 4: Advanced Game

My basic idea is that programming is the most powerful medium of developing the sophisticated and rigorous thinking needed for mathematics, for grammar, for physics, for statistics, for all the "hard" subjects.... In short, I believe more than ever that programming should be a key part of the intellectual development of people growing up. – Seymour Papert

Concepts learnt in this Unit:

- Relational operators (=, <, >)
- Variables as remote control
- Built-in variables - properties
- Motion - direction and bouncing

Chapter 4.1: Variables for Remote Control

Relational operators (=, <, >):

These operators compare two values and return true or false, depending on whether the comparison succeeded or failed. For example:

20 = 30 would return false

51 > -1 would return true, and so on.

These operators are typically used by conditional statements, such as, IF, Repeat until, etc.

We will take two variables "andy" and "tony" to represent ages of Andy and Tony, and see how the relational operators can be used to compare them:

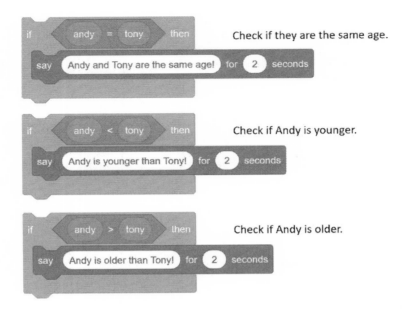

The "=" operator can also be used to compare strings:

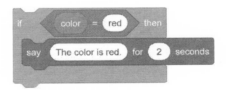

Variables as remote control:

This concept is best explained through an example.

Let us say we have a spinning wheel as shown below:

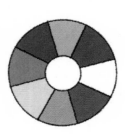
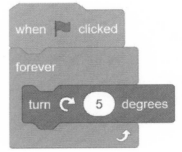

If we wanted to change the speed of this wheel, we would need to change the input of the "turn" command. Instead of manually changing the number, we could use a variable in place of this input:

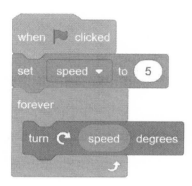

Now, whenever the variable "speed" changes, the spinning speed will also change immediately. So, the variable has become a "remote control" of the spinning wheel.

If you create button sprites labeled "Faster" and "Slower" with scripts as shown below, you will see how the remote control works:

Replacing fixed numbers (called "constants") with variables like this is also known as "parameterization".

Review questions:

1. What will the following script do?

   a) Say "You win" if score is less than 100
   b) Say "You win" if score is more than 100
   c) Say "You win" if score is less than or equal to 100
   d) Say "You win" if score is equal to or more than 100

2. The "glide" command has 3 inputs: time, x value, and y value. Below, we have a script that makes the sprite jump up/down. If we wanted to remotely control how fast the jump is, which input should we replace with a variable?

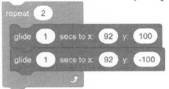

   a. The "time" input
   b. The "x value" input
   c. The "y value" input
   d. All inputs

Programming exercise:

Note: Look up http://abhayjoshi.net/scratch/book0/videos.htm to check out videos of sample solutions.

1. Write the above program to control a spinning wheel using variables. Include: start, stop, reverse, slow, and fast. Include upper/lower speed limits.

2. Modify your pong program (ball and single paddle) to add speed control. Add a slider variable to control the ball's speed. Count hits and misses.

Chapter 4.2: Built-in Variables and Bouncing

Variables - properties (built-in):

Scratch comes with many useful variables that provide some information about the sprites, the program itself, or something else. We call them *properties* to differentiate from variables that we create in the program.

For example, every sprite in your project has several properties; some examples are shown below. Their names clearly indicate what type of information they contain. For example, "x position" contains the current X coordinate of the sprite.

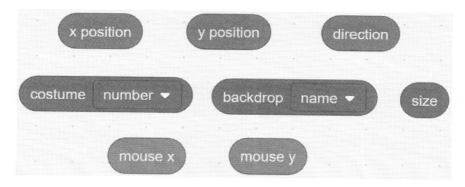

Properties can be used just like any other variable. For example, the command below will make the sprite move left or right where X=0.

Scratch also provides a way for one sprite to access information about other sprites through the following set of properties under the "Sensing" tab:

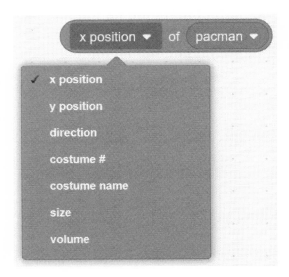

One big difference between your variables and properties is that properties are read-only; their values cannot be modified directly. For example, the "x position" property will change only when the sprite moves along the X axis.

Motion - direction and bouncing:
Generally speaking, whenever an object bounces off a flat surface, its incoming angle (with the surface) is equal to its outgoing angle. This is known as the "law of reflection".

Let's see how this works in Scratch, where angles of sprites are given by the "direction" property. A sprite's direction is measured with respect to the North direction. So, if the sprite is facing north, *direction* = 0. If it's facing east, *direction* = 90, and so on.

If you make a ball sprite bounce around the screen and observe how its "direction" property is affected by bouncing, you will notice the following:

1. When a sprite bounces off a vertical edge (left or right), the sprite's direction changes only in sign. So, 30 becomes -30, -110 becomes 110, and so on.
2. When a sprite with initial direction A bounces off a horizontal edge (top or bottom), after bouncing the sprite's direction becomes 180-A.

So, depending on what type of surface (horizontal or vertical) the sprite is bouncing off, the calculation of *direction* would be different.

Review questions:

1. A sprite's "direction" property is 180. That means, the sprite is pointing towards:
    a. North
    b. South
    c. East
    d. West

2. Assuming the sprite is at the center (i.e. at x=0, y=0) what will the following script do?

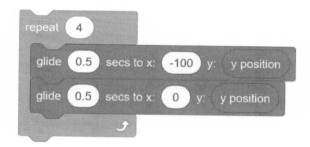

    a. Move the sprite up-down 4 times.
    b. Move the sprite diagonally 4 times.
    c. Move the sprite in a square around the center.
    d. Move the sprite left-right 4 times.

3. What will the following script do?

a. Make the sprite go continuously where the mouse pointer is.
b. Make the sprite go once where the mouse pointer is and then remain there.
c. Make the sprite move left-right only as the mouse pointer moves.
d. Make the sprite move up-down only as the mouse pointer moves.

4. When a ball bounces around the screen, its "direction" property changes only in sign every time it hits an edge. True or False?

5. A sprite's direction or orientation is a built-in Scratch variable. Which Scratch command SETS this variable?

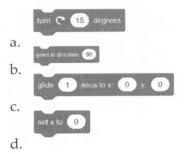

a.
b.
c.
d.

Programming practice:
Note: Look up http://abhayjoshi.net/scratch/book0/videos.htm to check out videos of sample solutions.

1. Write a program in which a bird flies in the sky continuously and the cat runs around on the ground exactly below the bird (in the hope to catch it).

2. Modify your Pong program that you wrote earlier and make the bouncing of the ball more realistic.

Chapter 4.3: Project Bricks

Project description:

This is a game you play with a ball and a flat paddle. A number of bricks are lined up at the top of the screen. As the ball bounces up and down you use the paddle to hit the bricks and score points. The ball must not touch the ground: after 3 such touches you lose the game. If you hit all the bricks you win the game. You can control the difficulty level of the game by changing the speed of the ball.

The following image will give you some more details of the game.

Brick sprites sit here until hit by the ball.

"Lives" shows number of remaining lives.

Controls speed of the ball.

Ball sprite moves up and down.

Paddle sprite moves left-right and makes the ball bounce.

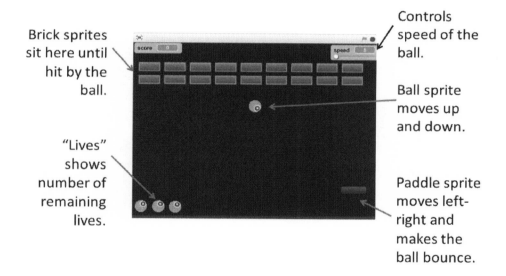

Sprites:
- Ball and paddle
- Bricks (10 or more, any shape)
- Number of lives

User Interaction:
- Green flag to reset everything.
- Speed slider to set the speed of the ball.
- SPACE BAR to start the game.

Additional requirements:
- Paddle should only move horizontally, should follow the mouse pointer
- A "score" variable should count # of bricks hit
- Screens should declare win or loss

Note: Look up http://abhayjoshi.net/scratch/book0/videos.htm to check out videos of sample solutions.

Write in your Design book:
- A short description of your project
- Answer these questions:
  1. What did you learn?
  2. What was exciting?
  3. What was challenging?

Unit 5: The Power of Variables

Technology is magic that you can use to do what you love,
if you learn to create. – Justin Richards

Concepts learnt in this Unit

- Arithmetic operators (+, -, *, /) and expressions
- User input (ASK)
- String variables
- String operations (join, letter, length of)
- Variables – as counters
- Random numbers
- Algorithms
- STAMP - creating images
- Conditional looping (repeat until)

Chapter 5.1: Arithmetic and Strings

Arithmetic operators (+, -, *, /) and expressions:

Under the "Operators" tab of Scratch, you will find the arithmetic operators:

All of us know these operators.

They can be used to create complex arithmetic expressions, such as, (20 + 3) x 5
(A – B) – ((C + D) / 10) where A, B, C, D are variables.

Equivalent Scratch expressions for these are shown below:

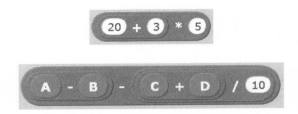

Be careful with the precedence of operations when you combine these operators. For example, if you wanted to perform (10 + (20 x 5)) you need:

And not:

User input (ASK):

Sometimes you may want to ask the user to provide some textual information. The ASK command presents a text window and waits. The user can type his/her reply in this text window and press ENTER. Whatever has been typed is then saved in the "ANSWER" variable. See the script below in which the user types "25" in the text window.

Before running the script: **answer**

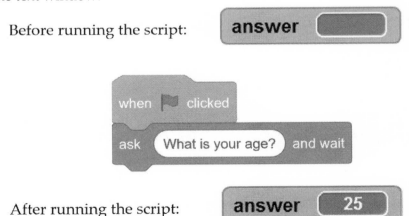

After running the script: **answer** 25

String variables:

The SET command (under "Data") stores a value in a variable. Earlier we saw that the value can be any number – negative or positive, whole or decimal. The value can also be a string of characters. For example, you can create a variable called "Name" and store the value "John Luke Pickard" in this variable.

Obviously, the CHANGE command will not work for a string of characters.

Here is an example of how a string variable may be used. We have a variable called "Message". In it we first store the string "Hello World". Then, the SAY command takes that string from the variable "message" and prints it on the screen.

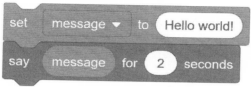

So, as you can see, you can use variables instead of actual values. When you refer to a variable in your script, the value stored inside that variable is used.

String variables can be modified by the "string operators" which we will consider next.

String operations:
A string is basically a sequence of alphanumeric letters:

The join operator allows you to concatenate two strings:

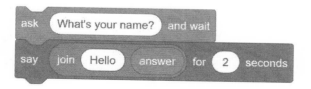

The above script asks you to type your name. If you type "George" the sprite will say "Hello George" on the screen.

The "letter" operator lets you get an individual letter of the given string:

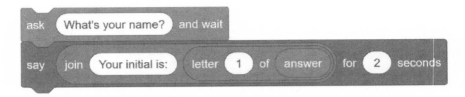

The above script asks you to type your name. If you type "Melinda" the sprite will say "Your initial is: M" on the screen.

The "length" operator tells you how many letters there are in the string:

The above script asks you to type your name. If you type "Devon" the sprite will say "Your name has 5 letters".

Review questions:
1. What will the following expression give?

    a. -190
    b. 860
    c. -300
    d. 570

2. What will "score" equal after we run the script below?

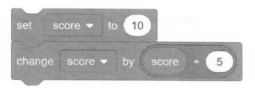

3. If the variable x contains 2000, what will the following expression return?

4. Assume that the "answer" property contains 100 before we run the following script. What will the variable "x" contain after we run this script?

    a. Whatever the user types in response to the ASK command.
    b. 100
    c. Whatever the user types in response to ASK only if it's a number.
    d. Unknown value

Programming practice:

Note: Look up http://abhayjoshi.net/scratch/book0/videos.htm to check out videos of sample solutions.

1. Write a simple calculator program that takes 2 numbers and performs basic arithmetic on them. Provide a button for each operation.

2. Write a program that converts Celsius to Fahrenheit and vice versa.

3. Ask for first, middle, last names, and then create full name and initials.

Chapter 5.2: Counters and Random Numbers

Variables – as counters:

In the script below, the variable "count" counts the number of repetitions:

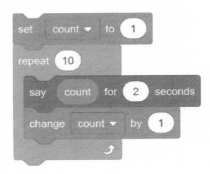

It essentially counts from 1 to 10. This is called a *counter*.

This very simple idea of using variables as counters actually has several interesting applications. For example, you could use a counter while "indexing" a string – i.e. act as a pointer to the letter being read in the string as you scan the string. Counters are also useful in combinatorial problems – for instance, a problem in which you may ask for "all prime numbers in the range 100 to 500."

Programming practice:

Note: Look up http://abhayjoshi.net/scratch/book0/videos.htm to check out videos of sample solutions.

1. Write a program that creates a comma-separated list of numbers. For example, if you provide 3, it will print 1,2,3; if you provide 5, it will print 1,2,3,4,5; and so on.

Random numbers:

Several outcomes (responses to events) in real life are unpredictable. Here are just a few examples:

```
Pick a ball out of a bag.
Roll a die.
Toss a coin.
Decide what to wear to a party.
```

Outcomes of these acts are not completely random; they are random within some constraints. The outcome in each of the above is one of a set of possible outcomes. Coin toss involves 2 possible outcomes; retrieving a ball from a bag depends on the number of balls in the bag; roll of a die has 6 possible outcomes, and so on.

Scratch offers a simple way to use randomness in programs through the following operator:

pick random 1 to 10

This operator returns a number from 1 to 10 – you can't predict what it will return. You can use any range (e.g. -100 to 100); the range can be in any order (e.g. 100 to -100); and it can even be a decimal range (e.g. 1.5 to 11.5).

The real key is to figure out how to use this simple operator to simulate the random events that you might want to use in your programs. For example, how would you simulate the roll of a die? Simple: use  since there are 6 possible outcomes.

Algorithms:

An *algorithm* is a step-by-step procedure that describes how a certain task can be performed. Strictly speaking, an algorithm has a formal structure (sometimes called the *pseudo-code*), which includes the initial and final states of the procedure, description of all inputs and the output, and so on. But, for the purpose of the programming projects in this book, we use algorithms rather loosely to create an informal *high-level description* of program steps, and help us in the process of creating the final Scratch scripts.

Here is an algorithm for a problem in day-to-day life: Let's say we have 3 opaque bottles and one and only one of them contains salt. We need to find out which one. Let's assume all three bottles contain stuff that is eatable (i.e. not harmful to taste!).

Algorithm:
```
Arrange the 3 bottles in a row and name them A, B, and C.
Open A.
      If the stuff inside is powdery and white
            Taste some of it.
            If taste is salty
                  Declare that A is the salt bottle.
                  Stop work
            End-if
      End-if
Open B.
      If the stuff inside is powdery and white
            Taste some of it.
            If taste is salty
                  Declare that B is the salt bottle.
                  Stop work
            End-if
      End-if
Declare that C is the salt bottle. (No need to open and
taste because at least one bottle contains salt).
```

Here is an example for an arithmetic problem: Let's say we want to find out the largest among the given 3 integers.

Algorithm:
```
Given: P, Q, and R are 3 integers. "Temp" is a temporary variable.
Compare P and Q
      If P > Q
            Save P in Temp
      Else
            Save Q in Temp
      End-if
Compare R and Temp
      If R > Temp
            Save R in Temp
      End-if
Declare Temp as the largest number.
```

Here is an example from the world of Scratch:

Algorithm to make a *rainfall*: (the sprite is a raindrop)

```
Forever:
    Go to a random point on the top edge
    Face downward
    Become visible
    Fall slowly to the bottom
    Become invisible
    Wait for a random amount of time
End-forever
```

Resulting Scratch script:

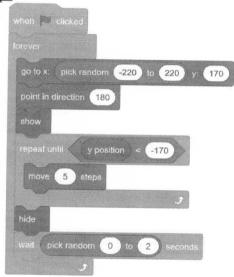

Review questions:

1. What will the following script do to the Cat sprite?

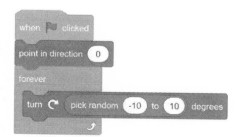

a) The cat will continuously turn, sometimes left sometimes right.
b) The cat will not turn because random will always return 0.
c) The cat will always turn clockwise because we have used the "Turn right" command.
d) The cat's direction property will always remain between -10 and 10.

2. In the following script we have 3 variables x, y, z which get set to random numbers as shown below:

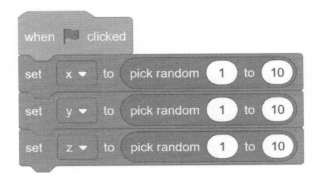

After clicking the Green flag, is it possible to have X=5, Y=5, Z=5?

a) No, because random always returns a different number.
b) Yes, because random may return any number in the given range.

3. See the script below. Which of the following letters is likely?

a. c
b. f
c. h
d. a

4. What range would you use in the RANDOM command to pick a month of the year?

5. If you wanted to use the "Go to x y" command to move your sprite such that it goes to any point at the top edge of the screen, what range would you use in the RANDOM command for the X value?

6. An algorithm is:
    a) A list of actions to perform, the order doesn't matter
    b) A sequence of conditional statements
    c) An ordered sequence of steps for carrying out a task
    d) Looping and conditions

7. Use a pencil/paper to follow the algorithm below. What will be drawn?
    Position the pencil at the top right part of the page
    Draw a horizontal line
    From the middle point of this line draw a vertical line downwards, until it reaches the bottom part of the page
    a) L
    b) C
    c) T
    d) I

Programming practice:
Note: Look up http://abhayjoshi.net/scratch/book0/videos.htm to check out videos of sample solutions.

2. Write a program in which a fortune-teller answers yes/no type of questions. For example, if you ask "Will I become the president?" the fortune-teller may answer "Maybe", or "Sure, why not!", or "No way!" etc. (Hint: The fortune-teller basically has a bag of ready answers.)

STAMP - creating images:

The STAMP command leaves an image of the sprite on the screen. See this example:

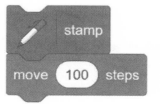

The first one is actually an image, and the second one is the sprite.

Although listed under the "Pen" tab, the STAMP command has no relation to the pen. So, to change the color of your image you must use the "change color effect" command. See the example below:

Once again, the first one is an image, and the second one is the sprite.

To erase the images created by STAMP, use the CLEAR command.

Review questions:
8. Which of the following is true?
    a. The stamp command modifies the appearance of the sprite.
    b. The stamp command paints the sprite's image onto the stage.
    c. The image created by stamp gets cleared when the program stops.
    d. The image created by stamp can be moved using motion commands.

Programming practice:
Note: Look up http://abhayjoshi.net/scratch/book0/videos.htm to check out videos of sample solutions.

3. Surprise flower: Upon every click of the pointer, a new flower comes up on the screen where you clicked. (Tip: Use multiple flower sprites, and then choose size and color randomly before every STAMP.)
4. Russian roulette: This program implements a simplified version of the Russian Roulette in casinos. There is a circle with each quadrant of a different solid color. A pointer is attached at the center of the circle. There are 4 buttons for each color. User clicks on one of these buttons, which causes the pointer to spin a random amount. If its tip stops in the color that the user picked, he makes money, else he loses.

Chapter 5.3: Project Falling Objects

Ok, it's time for another interesting project that will allow us to apply all the new ideas we learnt so far. But, before we discuss the project, let's just do one more new idea!

Conditional looping (repeat until):

In the simple looping covered earlier (Repeat and Forever), the repeat count is fixed beforehand. But, many times we may want to terminate the repetition based on a *condition*. For example, see the script below:

In this script, we want the user to enter his/her age. But, what if he/she enters a negative number? In order to ensure the age is a positive number, we need to continue asking the same question to the user until the user enters it correctly. "Repeat until" does exactly that: it asks the same question until age > 0.

Review questions:

1. How long will the following script run?

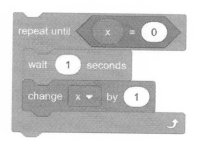

    a. 5 seconds
    b. 6 seconds
    c. 0 seconds
    d. forever

Programming project: Falling objects

In this game, some objects fall from the sky and the goal is for someone on the ground to catch as many as possible. All kinds of ideas are possible: catching gold coins, apples, raindrops, aliens, etc. The collecting sprite moves by following the mouse pointer or thru the left-right arrow keys.

Requirements:
- Use your own idea of falling objects in the sky.
- Use: if-else, broadcasting, sensing, user interaction, random.
- Give suitable names to your sprites (instead of sprite1, sprite2, etc).
- Objects must fall from random locations from the top so the catcher cannot predict where the next object will come from.
- Use variables to track points and/or # of attempts.
- Use the "h" key to show help, "Green flag" to set things up, and "Space bar" to start the game.

Note: Look up http://abhayjoshi.net/scratch/book0/videos.htm to check out videos of sample solutions.

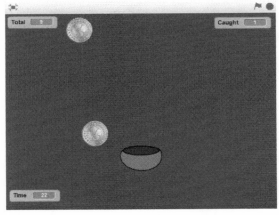

Write in your Design book:
- A short description of your project
- Answer these questions:
  1. What did you learn?
  2. What was exciting?
  3. What was challenging?

Unit 6: Clones

Don't just consume things. Create things. Take some time to learn the technologies that touch every part of our life. That's how you can prepare yourself for the skills you need for your future. – Barack Obama

Concepts learnt in this Unit

- Basics of object oriented programming (OOP)
- Creating instances using clones
- Motion – piggybacking another object

Chapter 6.1: Clones

OOP - creating instances using clones:

OOP stands for "object oriented programming". In OOP, there is a concept of a "class", which defines the characteristics (i.e. properties and actions) of a collection of identical objects, and an object is an instance of that class. For example, "Tiger" could be a class with properties such as "height" and "weight" and actions such as "growling" and "hunting". And then an actual tiger that is 4 feet tall and 300 pound heavy tiger would be an instance of this class. Loosely speaking, we can also think of a class as "parent" and objects as its progeny – children, grandchildren, etc.

Using this idea, a running program can have multiple instances of a class.

From Scratch's perspective, every sprite can be viewed as a class which contains its own data (variables) and methods (scripts). And the idea of creating instances of a class is implemented using a feature called "clones". So, clones are basically identical copies of a sprite that exist only at run-time, that is, they are created by the program and they vanish when the program stops running.

The following command allows a sprite to create a clone of itself:

A sprite can create clones of other sprites too, as shown below:

A clone inherits (gets its own copy of) all scripts of its parent sprite except the ones that begin with the event "When Green Flag clicked". In addition, every clone, when it is created, runs (only once) scripts that start with the following event:

All clones are deleted (i.e. they vanish) when you stop the program using the STOP ALL command or by clicking the STOP button. Each clone may also delete itself using this command:

delete this clone

Although a clone is an identical copy of a sprite, it does not *share* the parent's private variables: instead, each clone gets its own copy of all private variables. For example, if the parent sprite has a private variable called "id", the clone would also have its own private variable called "id".

Similarly, the clone also gets its own copies of built-in sprite-specific Scratch properties such as, *xposition* and *yposition*.

Review questions:

1. Let's say a sprite creates a clone. After creating the clone, if the parent's direction changes from 90 to 180, the clone's direction will also change to 180.
    a. True
    b. False

2. Let's say a sprite has the following two scripts.

   If another sprite sends a broadcast message:
    a. Parent as well as all the 10 clones will say "Hello".
    b. Only the 10 clones will say "Hello".
    c. Only the parent sprite will say "Hello".
    d. Results are unpredictable, there is no "When I start as a clone" script.

Programming practice:

Note: Look up http://abhayjoshi.net/scratch/book0/videos.htm to check out videos of sample solutions.

1. Write a program in which bubbles or balloons continuously pop up from the ground (from random locations) and float up to the top and then disappear. Use clones to create this multiplicity of bubbles (or balloons). Use a counter to track the number of "live" bubbles at any instant.

2. Modify the "falling object" program you wrote in a previous unit and use the idea of clones for the falling objects.

3. Modify your earlier "Bricks" game to use a single brick sprite which clones itself to create multiple bricks.

Chapter 6.2: Game of Flappy Bird

Piggyback motion:

When you design animation in Scratch, there are instances when you want one sprite to "ride" another sprite, i.e. track another sprite's motion. For example, consider a horse-rider. Or consider an animation in which a person gets into a bus, drives to downtown, gets off and walks to his office. Such "riding" or "tracking" motion is called piggyback motion.

Achieving this piggyback effect is quite straightforward. You basically want one sprite (say sprite2) to track the motion of another sprite (say sprite1). Motion comprises the x and y coordinates and direction. The following properties can be used to access these values.

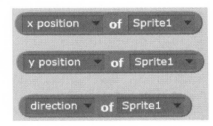

And sprite2 can use the following commands to continuously track the motion of sprite1.

In order to ensure sprite2 appears at the right place on top of sprite1, you may need to adjust the x and y values slightly by using the arithmetic operators.

Here is an example of sprite2 piggybacking sprite1:

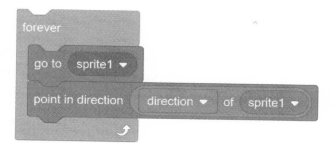

"Flappy bird" Project Specification:

In this game project there is a flying bird, which "appears" to fly continuously to the left, and there are pairs of vertical bars (or pipes) with a small gap between them, that move from left to right. Each pair of pipes is exactly aligned vertically. The gap in each pair appears at a random height. The objective of the game is to make the bird move through the gap between the pipes. If the bird touches any of the pipes, the bird dies and the game is over. The bird can be moved upward/downward using the up/down arrow keys. The player is scored based on the number of pipes that the bird successfully passes through.

The following image shows the main screen of this game.

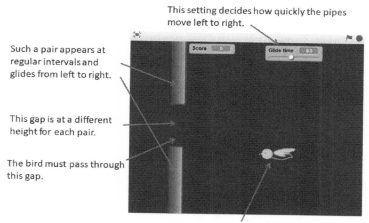

Design:
Use the following checkpoints and hints to design this program:

Checkpoint 1:
1. Get a flying bird facing west that flaps its wings.
    *   Arrow keys will move it up and down
2. Get two vertical pipes ("upper" and "lower"):
    *   Make them as tall as the screen
    *   Make "upper" travel from the left edge to the right edge repeatedly, and use "score" variable to count repetitions
    *   Set Y position of "upper" randomly
    *   Align "lower" vertically with "upper" with a small gap between them and synchronize its motion with "upper".
3. Bird should sense touching both pipes.
    *   If it touches any of the pipes, it falls down and the game stops.

Checkpoint 2:
1. Add a "help" screen and start game with "space bar pressed" event
2. Add "Glide time" slider variable to control pipe speed.
3. Use clones to create "upper" and "lower" pipes:
    *   "upper" parent will create a clone every few seconds (at random)
    *   The clone will: a) Save its Y position in a variable, b) Signal "lower" pipe and start moving
    *   "lower" parent will create a clone when signaled by "upper"
    *   The clone will calculate its Y position and start moving.

Note: Look up http://abhayjoshi.net/scratch/book0/videos.htm to check out videos of sample solutions.

Write in your Design book:
*   A short description of your project
*   Answer these questions:
    1. What did you learn?
    2. What was exciting?
    3. What was challenging?

Unit 7: Procedures and Pen Art

Computer literacy must also mean the ability to do computing, and not merely to recognize, identify, or be aware of alleged facts about computing. – Arthur Luehrmann

Concepts learnt in this Unit

- Pen commands
- Basic Turtle geometry
- Custom Procedures
- Custom Procedures with inputs
- Abstraction
- Drawing a circle
- Scratch Turbo mode

Chapter 7.1: Pen Art

Pen commands:

Every sprite in Scratch has a pen attached to it (at its center) and is able to draw on the background. The pen commands are listed under the "Pen" tab and they contain commands to put the pen down (after which the sprite will start drawing wherever it goes), pen up (after which the drawing will stop), set pen size, set pen color, and so on.

The actual drawing happens when the sprite moves using the motion commands. Using cleverly designed scripts, you can draw practically any type of geometric patterns. For example, the following script draws a pentagon:

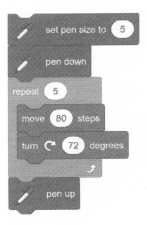

The pen commands listed under the "Pen" tab help you perform various operations on the pen itself, such as set or change its size, color, and shade. Most of these commands are self-explanatory.

Refer to the book *Pen Art for Scratch Programmers* written by the same author for a more detailed treatment of Scratch's Pen capability and for numerous interesting programming problems.

Custom Procedures:

A Scratch *instruction* consists of a combination of one or more command blocks that we drag and drop in the script area, and which is then run by Scratch when we click on it. For example, the following is an instruction which evaluates the expression 20*30 and shows 600 on the screen.

A Scratch instruction, like the one above, always carries out a specific, well-defined, and repeatable task. If you look carefully, you will notice that the instruction above contains the keyword "SAY" and the symbol "*" (for multiplication). Each of these words or symbols is called a Scratch *procedure*. In other words, every Scratch instruction consists of one or more Scratch procedures.

A *procedure* is like a recipe of how to do something. For example, the MOVE command is a procedure that knows how to move a sprite. Several Scratch blocks are thus individual procedures that carry out specific tasks.

Scratch allows you to define your own procedures. Go to the "More blocks" tab and click on "Make a block". The following picture shows that I am creating a new procedure called "Greeting".

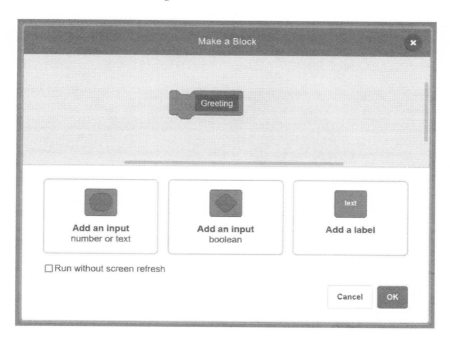

When you click Ok, you see this new block in the script area:

Below this you create a script by attaching existing Scratch command blocks. This is what I created:

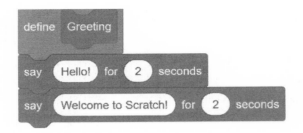

You now have a new procedure called "Greeting" which you can use in any script. For example:

Review questions:

1. What will the following script draw?

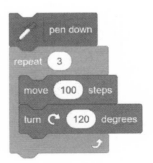

    a. Straight line
    b. Three parallel lines
    c. Equilateral triangle
    d. Incomplete square with 3 sides

2. What will the following script draw?

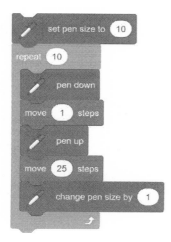

a. A series of equal size dots.
b. A series of dots of increasing size.
c. A series of dots of decreasing size.
d. A straight line.

3. See the Scratch command below. What is it?

   a. An instruction
   b. A procedure
   c. Neither instruction nor procedure
   d. Both instruction and procedure

4. The following script shows the definition of a new procedure called "jump". How can I use this new procedure in my Scratch program?

a. By clicking anywhere on this definition
b. By sending a broadcast "jump"

c. By using the new block   in my script
d. By saving this definition in a separate project

Programming practice:

Note: Look up http://abhayjoshi.net/scratch/book0/videos.htm to check out videos of sample solutions.

1. Write programs that draw the following patterns using repetition. **Hint**: Each design involves a repeating pattern. Once you identify the basic pattern, you can just use the REPEAT command.

Chapter 7.2: Procedures with Inputs

Custom Procedures with inputs:

The behavior of many procedures depends on how they are invoked. It depends on the *input* supplied. So, [move ⬤ steps] can do its job only when you tell it *how many* steps to move. Or, [wait ⬤ seconds] command needs to know *how many* seconds to wait.

Scratch allows you to define your own procedures which take input. Right-click the new block "Jump" (which we defined earlier) and click "edit". Click on "Options" and you will see the following:

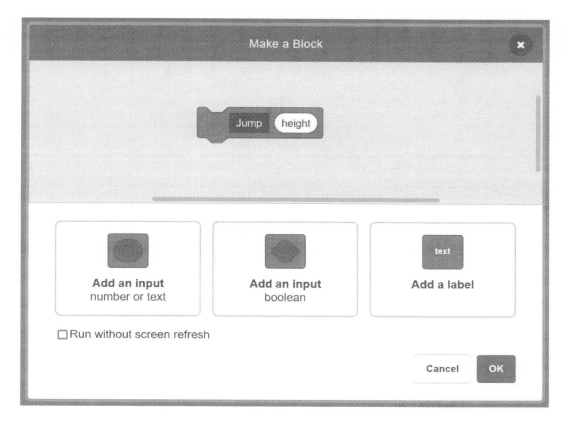

We will add to "Jump" a *number* input labelled as "height". The label has no importance really, other than giving a descriptive name to the input.

After clicking OK, you will see the following:

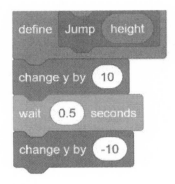

Now, the input is useful only if it is actually used in the procedure. You can drag the new input and use it wherever appropriate in your sequence of commands. This is how our final "jump" procedure will look:

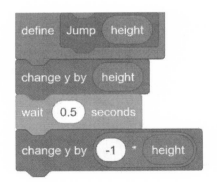

If I use this new procedure in a script, say, as   , the sprite will jump up and down by 100 steps.

Abstraction:

Abstraction is an interesting concept which means capturing a (relatively) complex idea into a single word (or phrase), image, map, audio clip, etc. Even in our day-to-day life we assign words to complex concepts or ideas. For example, "pedestrian" is an abstraction for *a person walking on a footpath*. Once we assign such words to ideas, we refer to the ideas simply thru those words.

Similarly, your new Scratch procedure "Jump" is the abstraction for the idea of moving a sprite some distance up and down. Defining a new word which has a specific meaning is called abstraction.

Review questions:

1. Every Scratch procedure requires input. True or False?
2. You can define a new Scratch procedure that takes more than one input. True or False?
3. A sprite has a new procedure called "Square" as shown below. Which of the following is true?

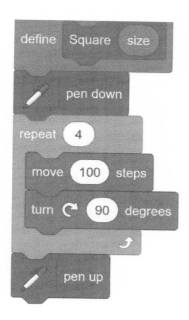

a. It will draw a square as big as the input "size".
b. It will not draw anything.
c. It will draw a square of size 100.
d. It will not draw a square but a set of 4 connected lines.

Programming practice:

1. Modify the drawing program you wrote earlier (in Chapter 7.1) and create procedures for "square wave", "staircase", and "point star" such that each of them accepts appropriate input. For example, "staircase" will have 2 inputs: one for size and the other for number of stairs.

2. Using procedure blocks that use input, draw the following shapes. **Hint**: Design your basic shape to accept inputs for size and color.

Chapter 7.3: Going in Circles

Drawing a circle:

A circle is drawn when the pen moves and turns continuously. So the following script would draw a circle of length (circumference) 360.

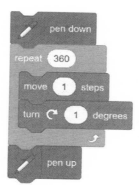

In reality, this script does not draw a circle; it draws a polygon with 360 sides each of length 1. But, for all practical purposes it looks like a circle. In fact, if you experiment a bit, you will discover that polygons of even less number of sides (say 180 or 100) also look like circles on the screen. But, remember that the total angle must always be 360 degrees.

Next, we can use the following formula that relates diameter of a circle to its circumference and come up with a Scratch procedure to draw a circle of the given diameter.

Diameter = Circumference / 3.14159

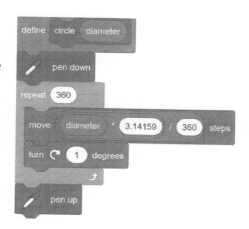

So, "circle 50" will draw a circle of diameter 50; "circle 150" will draw a circle of diameter 150; "circle 200" will draw a circle of diameter 200; and so on.

Scratch Turbo mode:

Every motion command in Scratch takes a very short but finite time. This time actually helps in creating smooth animation because we can break down a long jump into multiple smaller jumps and then the series of jumps creates the impression that the sprite is moving smoothly.

For example, the script below makes the sprite turn slowly around itself.

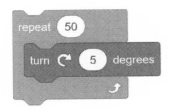

But, this delay can be problematic for some other occasions. For example, if you are drawing a complicated drawing, say a spiral, the number of moves is quite large and so, the cumulative delay can make the drawing really slow. For such purposes, you can practically eliminate the delay by using the "turbo" mode (click "Edit" and then click "Turbo mode"). Suddenly you will notice that your drawing has become much quicker.

With turbo mode on, the following two scripts will be identical in behavior.

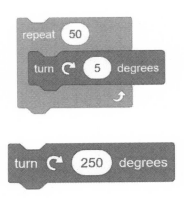

Review questions:

1. The following script is expected to draw a polygon of 180 edges. How much should the input to the "Turn" command be?

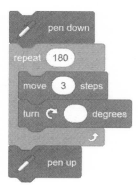

    a. 1

    b. 2

    c. 4

    d. 180

Programming practice:

1. Using the "circle" procedure block defined above, draw the following shapes.

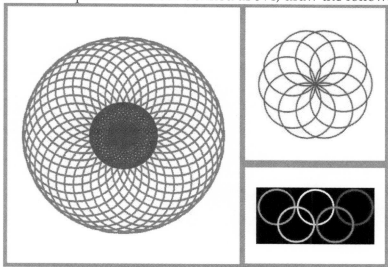

Chapter 7.4: Project Traffic Light

Description:

Draw (using pen, NOT paint editor) a traffic light as shown and animate it, i.e. make the lights go ON and OFF at regular intervals.

Add a two-way multi-lane highway and show one or more moving cars that move in each direction continuously but obey the traffic light, i.e. they slow down when the light is amber, stop when it is red, and move when it is green.

Additional requirements:

- As mentioned, the traffic light is not a sprite, but is drawn by the program using pen commands.
- Define the following procedures:
  - "Fdcircle" procedure will draw a filled circle of the given diameter. The caller will choose the color. (Hint: "pendown" draws a dot the size of the pen)
  - "Frectangle" procedure will draw a filled rectangle of the given height and width. The caller will choose the color.
  - "Traffic.Light" will draw the full traffic light. It will take the diameter of each light as input and calculate all other dimensions accordingly.
- Create two separate versions of the program:
  - In one, use only "broadcasting" to coordinate the interaction between the traffic light and the moving cars.
  - In the other, use only "variables" to coordinate the interaction between the traffic light and the moving cars.
- Optional: Have a separate traffic light for each direction.

Unit 8: Additional CS Concepts

Now more people are doing work that requires individual decision-making and problem-solving, and we need an educational system that will help develop those skills. – Seymour Papert

These are additional and slightly advanced concepts that you could use for cool projects such as the ones demonstrated in the book "Advanced Scratch Programming" by the same author. By all means learn these concepts and apply them in your own interesting projects, or refer to the projects listed in this book.

Recursion:

The idea of recursion is a property of procedures. Simply stated, a recursive procedure calls itself. For example, the following procedure is recursive:

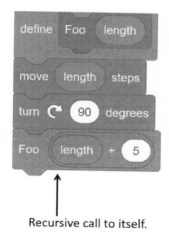

Recursive call to itself.

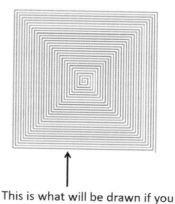

This is what will be drawn if you call this procedure.

If you call this procedure, say by using ![Foo 1], it will draw a rectangular spiral forever; it will never return because it will call itself indefinitely. What you will have is a program that will run forever!

Writing a program that never terminates is interesting but not very convenient. We would like to write recursive programs that do interesting things and terminate (i.e. stop) when their job is done. The Scratch command

stop this script ▼ will stop the currently running procedure and return to the calling procedure. Thus, the infinite recursion will be broken.

Here is a modified recursive procedure that will not run forever:

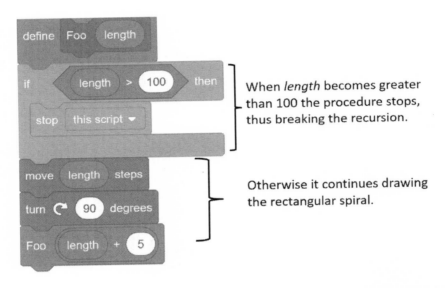

When *length* becomes greater than 100 the procedure stops, thus breaking the recursion.

Otherwise it continues drawing the rectangular spiral.

There is another, more general, way to make recursion finite, that is, make it stop after some time. We can simply decide how deep the recursion should go. See the modified Foo procedure below:

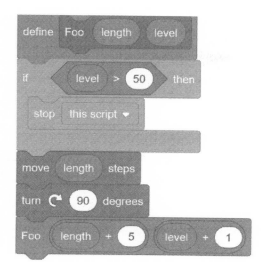

Here, let's assume *level* = 1 when we call Foo. It becomes 2 when Foo is called the 2nd time. It becomes 3 when Foo is called the 3rd time, and so on. "IF" will cause this recursive chain to terminate when *level* becomes 51.

Programming practice:

1. We used recursion above to draw a rectangular spiral. Modify your script to draw the following recursive patterns. As indicated, you just need to modify the turning angle.

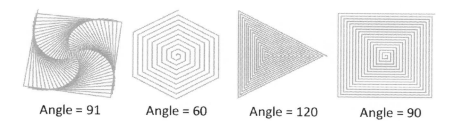

| Angle = 91 | Angle = 60 | Angle = 120 | Angle = 90 |

2. Refer to the chapter on "Recursion" in *Pen Art in Scratch Programming* and try to do the programming assignments given in that chapter.

List data structure:
A list is a type of data storage that stores multiple pieces of information: words, numbers, or sentences.

Click on "Make a List" under "Data" to create a new empty list variable, and then use the following commands to manipulate the list.

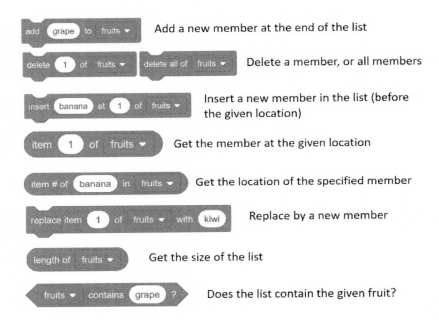

Add a new member at the end of the list

Delete a member, or all members

Insert a new member in the list (before the given location)

Get the member at the given location

Get the location of the specified member

Replace by a new member

Get the size of the list

Does the list contain the given fruit?

Here is an example script that shows how the members of a list can be listed:

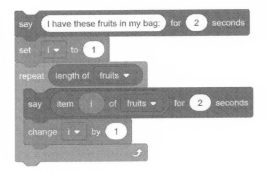

124

The following condition checks if the given item is present in the list:

Programming practice:
Note: Look up http://abhayjoshi.net/scratch/book0/videos.htm to check out videos of sample solutions.

3. Convert a sentence into individual words and then say it in the reverse order. For example, if the user gives "My name is Buddy" the program should say "Buddy is name My".

Boolean logic operators (AND, OR, NOT):
Conditions, i.e. questions that return yes/no or true/false, can be combined using these logic operators, also known as "Boolean" operators. For example, in the script below, the sprite will say "We must be in heaven!" only if the temperature is in the range 60 to 90.

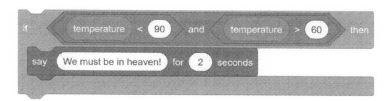

The best way to understand how the logic operators work is to construct "truth tables" as shown below.

The AND operator

Condition 1	Condition 2	Combined effect (output)
False	False	False
False	True	False
True	False	False
True	True	True

As you can see, the output is true only when both conditions are true.

The OR operator

See this example:

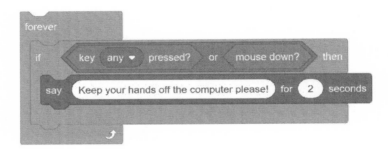

This script checks if you are pressing any key or clicking the mouse pointer.

Condition 1	Condition 2	Combined effect (output)
False	False	False
False	True	True
True	False	True
True	True	True

As you can see, the output is true when at least one condition is true.

The NOT operator
See this example:

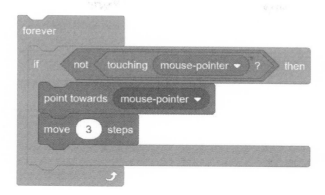

NOT negates the given condition. So for a NOT expression to be True, the condition must be False. In the script above, the sprite will move towards the mouse pointer continuously but stop moving when it is touching the pointer.

Condition	Combined effect (output)
False	True
True	False

As you can see, the output is the exact opposite of the input.

Programming practice:
Note: Look up http://abhayjoshi.net/scratch/book0/videos.htm to check out videos of sample solutions.

4. When the mouse pointer touches your cat sprite, it meows. It meows only once after touching. If you remove the pointer away and touch again, it meows again.

Nested conditional statements:

The IF (and the IF-Else) command can be used in many variations. One variation called "nested IF" is shown below. Nested IF means having one IF command inside another.

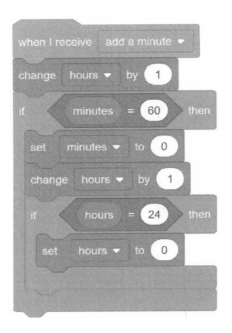

This script is for a digital clock. It adds a minute to the time.

If the total minutes become 60, that's counted as an hour and counting of minutes starts again from 0.

If the total hours become 24, counting starts again from 0.

Mapping random numbers to a set of things:

Sometimes you want to pick something from a collection of things, which is not necessarily an ordered list of numbers. For example, you want to pick a color from the set of 4 colors: green, red, blue, and yellow. How would you do that using the random operator?

Well, the first step is to realize that the collection contains 4 items. So we should use `pick random 1 to 4` to pick from 4 numbers. Next, we can map each number to a color: so, 1 could map to red, 2 to blue, 3 to yellow, and 4 to green. Then, depending on what *pick random* returned, you would know which color to pick. Here is the script to show the entire scheme of things:

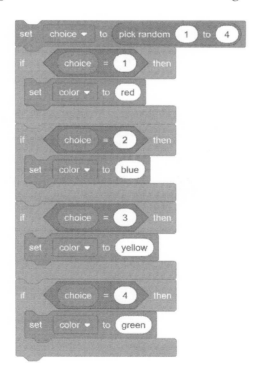

Mouse events using polling:

Similar to keyboard interaction, mouse signals are handled in two ways: one is called events (or "interrupt driven") as shown below:

The other is called "polling" as shown below:

If you want to check this continuously you must use a forever loop:

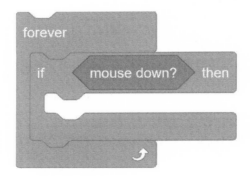

Note that the condition is "mouse down" and not "mouse click".

It is possible in the "polling" method that some mouse-downs might be missed if their timing does not match with when the IF command checks for the mouse-down. Also, polling (in a Forever loop) runs continuously taking CPU time, whereas event handlers do not take CPU time, because they sleep and are "woken up" when the event occurs. But the advantage of polling is that the program has full control on when to handle mouse signals. When the program stops, polling also stops, whereas event handlers would run even if the program has stopped.

Another interesting advantage of polling is that you can combine multiple events using logic operators as shown below:

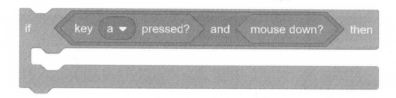

User input validation:

The ASK command allows the user to enter input, which could be words or numbers. For example, you might ask the user to enter his/her height. It is essential to ensure that the user enters a valid input, in this case, a valid height. Something like -50 or "abc" would not be a valid height.

The program must have a way to validate the user input, and if it is not valid, go back and ask again. The following example shows how this can be done:

Let's say we ask the use for his/her age. We assume that the age cannot be less than 1 or more than 100.

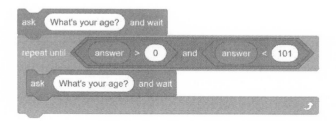

The loop continues to ask the same question until the user gives a valid answer.

Variables scope - local/global:

When you create a variable, you get the following dialog box:

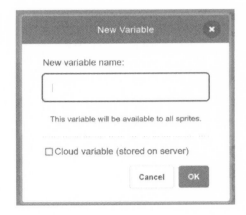

Below the name, there are two options to select from: (1) For all sprites, and (2) For this sprite only. If you select the first option, you create a "global" variable, and if you select the second option, you create a "local" variable.

A global variable is visible to all sprites in your project. Any sprite can set it, change it, or use it. On the other hand, a local variable is visible only to this sprite (one in which you created it).

It is a good practice to decide the scope of each variable carefully, and make it "global" only if it is clearly going to be used by multiple sprites. For example, the "score" variable in a "pacman" game would be needed by multiple sprites (prizes, pacman, obstacles, etc.) so it should be "global".

A local variable, if displayed, uses a different notation. See below:

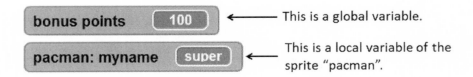

Using variables as gates:

There are occasions when the user must not be allowed to start playing the game until some setup is completed. For example, let's say your game starts when the SPACE key pressed. But, before pressing the SPACE key the user must set a few things, for example, slider variables. We can enforce this by using the concept of "using variables as gates". In the example below, we will use a variable called "setupdone" which will be False initially and True after setup is done.

Set the variable to False initially.

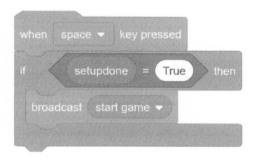

Start the game (by sending broadcast) only when set up is done. The variable will be set to True by whoever is in charge of setup.

Variables - as timer:

The combination of variables and the WAIT command can be used to implement a timer. See the script below:

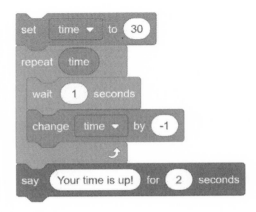

The "time" variable is set in the beginning to whatever value you want to set for your game. The repeat loop then decrements it a second at a time until it becomes 0.

It may be confusing to see the "time" variable getting decremented and also being used in the REPEAT command. The REPEAT command uses its initial value (in this case 30) to decide the number of repetitions.

A more intuitive (and less confusing) way to do this might be:

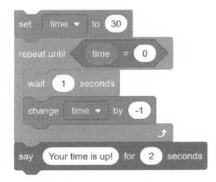

Made in the USA
Middletown, DE
23 September 2022

10816459R00080